Cultural Leadership

Cultural Leadership
The New Chemistry of Leading Differently

B. Stewart

ISBN-13: 978-1456335908
ISBN -10: 1456335901

To my mother, Carolyn Stewart

Contents

Introduction

Great books usually set out to answer one central question; the more basic the question, the more powerful the answer. For example, noted anthropologist Jared Diamond, author of the Pulitzer Prize–winning book *Guns, Germs, and Steel*, set out to answer a very basic question, "Why are Western countries generally more wealthy than nonwestern countrie" After twenty years of research he narrowed the answer down to one simple answer: geographical luck. This book sets out to answer another basic question, "What is the best model of leadership in a new world of increasing diversity, complexity, and rapid change?" After reviewing current leadership models and theories, I quickly realized the model of leadership I was looking for did not exist.

I was beginning to think I was completely alone in my theory until I came across an article published in *Scientific American* magazine on the new psychology of leadership. This article, written by Stephen D. Reicher, Michael J. Platow, and S. Alexander Haslam, articulated a fresh view of leadership. This, along with my deeply held prior convictions, became the social foundation for a new leadership concept: cultural leadership. This concept is grounded in the latest social research connecting the three major schools of leadership thought: the trait school, the situational school, and the transformational charismatic school. But the social identity perspective is not enough; it lacks the global scientific research foundation required to be relevant across multiple cultures. This is where the GLOBE (Global

Leadership and Organizational Behavior Effectiveness research project) studies at the Wharton School became invaluable. Their research, conducted over twenty years in most major countries, for the first time provides a clear cross-cultural perspective, along with data about which leadership traits (skills) are transcendent, culturally specific, and negatively viewed in all cultures. The GLOBE conclusions became the research foundation for my new model of cultural leadership.

The final piece of this new model was to understand the essence of truly effective leadership—not the traditional functions, but what is really critical in a leadership role. Of course we know leaders create vision, inspire, and carry out all the other charismatic components, but how is a leader truly successful? I came to the following realization: a leader's essential role is to create coalitions of followers to achieve organizational goals. How is this done? By deeply understanding the characteristics of followers, and reflecting or mirroring those characteristics back to followers in an inspiring, motivational, and culturally intelligent way. Once again, to be culturally relevant, successful leaders must know: how culture is created, its essential components, and how to sustain it. And most important, they must know how to transport this skill from one cultural domain to another without losing effectiveness.

Every organization, even the smallest, has cliques and clans. It is my contention that the key to an organization is not the individual, but the clique. Cliques are a small group of individuals who shape and influence the perceptions, feelings, attitudes, and values of one another. Conversely, a clan is a group of no more than 150 people who share a common goal and function. Clans are distinguished by their common logo, identity, and general agreement on cultural and social views. Building coalitions of cliques and clans to achieve organizational goals and objectives is a leader's primary task.

Connectivity is the key strategy that leaders can use to build strong coalitions, which in turn create cultural chemistry that invariably leads to success. Successful leaders, in a world of ever-increasing globalization, possess a keen ability to form coalitions of supporters that represent a wide range of divergent mind-sets, geographic identity, and perspectives. They inspire supporters, but also utilize seven activators (more about the seven activators later) needed to connect and mobilize followers to action. This is the chemistry created when divergent minds act in unison to achieve a cause.

Again, transportable chemistry is the idea that cultural leaders, by connecting with their followers, create a certain type of chemistry that mobilizes followers to act in unison. The more people act in unison, the more chemistry is created. This is because we are social animals by nature and herd animals by action. We draw energy from being a part of the crowd. Crowds have the effect of releasing dopamine into our system, stimulating a feeling of elation. This is why many of us possess lasting memories of working in a place where everyone was on the same team, working toward a common goal. Unison is addictive.

Creating cultural chemistry is best understood by acknowledging the uniqueness of every organizational culture. Just as each individual has a unique DNA, organizational cultures have unique cultural DNA, which ultimately determines the success of the organization. There are four elements of this cultural DNA: the human element, the network element, the system element, and the leadership element. Each of these elements plays a primary role in shaping an organization's unique cultural DNA. Special leaders successfully improve the health of their organizations when they focus on connecting with each of the cultural DNA elements. For instance, when leaders connect with the individual human element, they create commitment. When they connect with the network element, they generate cooperation through collaboration. When they connect with the systems element, they improve coordination. And when they connect with themselves, they exude credibility. So when followers are committed around a cause, they cooperate with each other through collaboration, synchronize their actions through coordination, and are connected to their leader. This is an organization destined to succeed.

I believe this book provides thoughtful concepts on how to effectively reach far beyond the boundaries of traditional leadership into the wide open spaces of the transportable chemistry of cultural leadership—the kind of chemistry that connects to anybody, anytime, anywhere.

Section 1:

The New Global Leadership

Chapter 1

Transportable Chemistry

Leadership in Motion

The only thing more difficult than finding a needle in a haystack is finding a particular piece of hay in the same haystack. Why? Chemistry: the interchangeable properties making one out of many. Chemistry is powerful in its ability to assimilate; transportable chemistry is infinitely more powerful in its ability to transform. To better understand the impact of transportable chemistry, we will examine the leadership approach of Osama bin Laden, discuss the source of Hitler's power, and learn some of the key leadership secrets of our most recent presidents.

This is where transportable chemistry gets interesting. Each human group represents a culture; each culture represents an archive of transferrable, institutionalized teachings, myths, and observations. The instinct of culture is impeccably accurate. This instinct ultimately invites into, or rejects from its ranks, any person who does not walk and talk authentically. Members within a culture have keen social antennae.

Culture is immensely sensitive. Culture hears, sees, and picks up on everything said or inferred.

Back to our haystack premise. The best contemporary example of transportable chemistry is the international terrorist Osama bin Laden. His ability to relate, change form, protect, and be protected since 2001 is uncanny. Why? It is because Osama bin Laden has so effectively changed his cultural rhetoric from "America hates me" to "America hates us." He has found protection in the unification of identity. He is the piece of hay in the haystack.

An objective analysis of bin Laden, his influence, and strategies has one conclusion: he is a cultural leader. Cultural leadership, the foundation of this book, is the most profound concept in modern leadership theory. Later, I will dig deeper into this diamond mine of a concept, but suffice it to say, cultural leadership is the end result of a robust process—a process that includes adaptation in real time. I call it transportable chemistry.

Transportable chemistry must operate covertly. Granted, we refer to "covert" in a different sense: not hiding, but revealing; not secret, but obvious; connecting to that which connects everybody, hiding in plain sight. But transportable chemistry is only half of the picture. The ultimate objective is relating not only to cliques, clans, coalitions, and categories, but doing so with anyone, spontaneously, at any time. The key factor is influence that is not physically bound to any single person, place, or group. When a leader accomplishes this, he inextricably combines destinies, and elevates those qualities previously viewed as irrelevant to a place of importance. This is precisely what bin Laden has done.

Al Qaeda is effective partly because its leader is one of them, in a sense; this turns each member into a leader. In this way, Osama bin Laden epitomizes cultural leadership. By synchronizing vision, bin Laden has transformed small, isolated regiments into a military force, and, with less than elite technology, has deftly fought the most powerful military in the world. Cultural leadership cannot be overestimated. It is the creation of powerful sandbags from powerless grains of sand.

How does one man in the mountains of Afghanistan hide from the most powerful and technologically robust nation? By having a deep insight, not only into the minds of his followers, but also into the minds of his competitors. For bin Laden, cultural leadership is the ultimate hiding place because it leverages chemistry, transports its connections, organizes individuals, and manages risk by equally valuing destiny. It is safe. When you reverse engineer bin Laden's effectiveness, invaluable lessons emerge.

Looks Can Be Deceiving

Notice something. Although bin Laden is very wealthy, he never wears a suit or even expensive mountain garb. He melds into his followers. His mannerisms and nonverbal comportment render him indistinguishable. Consequently, when his followers elevate him, they elevate themselves. There is a lesson there.

Much of what leaders have learned over the last fifty years of business and leadership training must be reevaluated—and some abandoned. How does a leader dress? What is a leader's communication style? Are these elements utilized to prove position worth, pay, or power? Think about it. Only you can answer. True cultural leadership is given, not taken; earned, not awarded. Whether your followers are church congregants or multiple Fortune 500 divisions, the most effective cultural leaders of the twenty-first century are hard to pick out of the corporate photo. They lead from within.

Our bin Laden discussion presents profound social implications because the world is changing, and the definition of what makes a cultural leader is changing, too. As I've discussed, transportable chemistry is one component, but it cannot be effective without a clear command of additional leadership tools.

Your ability to articulate, gather broad support, and execute vision will be directly associated with your mastery of cultural nuances. This is more than a multilingual construct, but rather an elegant skill of human discernment.

For any of this to occur, you must employ an honest examination of your preexisting business, interpersonal, and social philosophies in an effort to uncover cultural inefficiencies. Remember, nobody is born with broad international reach and cultural understanding. Cultural competency is acquired through experience, exposure, and being open to learning about differences—those things opposite you, opposite your upbringing, opposite your biases. This learning is not academic, because you can learn without understanding. This learning is an adolescent-like openness that processes purely without the convolution of personal filters.

Today, subtle vibrations of change are being felt across cultures and continents—a tremor, not fueled by greed-induced chaos but rather a global desire to relate beyond commerce, to unearth a human simplicity common to all, an indistinguishable connectedness. Harnessing this simplicity can be a complex cross-cultural endeavor. To effectively navigate these multicultural complexities requires a strategic framework of beliefs, practices, and protocols. To start, you must reject racial assumptions, ethnic stereotypes, and other unfounded cultural biases. Those who remain committed to such thinking choose to become irrelevant. I have identified seven activators that are not only essential to cultural leadership, but are vital tools in disassembling such outdated approaches:

- Foresight
- The ability to connect and engage
- Relevant communication
- Trustworthiness
- Dynamic presence
- Positive attitude
- Confidence builder

The strategic understanding and practice of these ideals will ultimately compound a leader's influence by broadening the reachable constituents. I expand on each of these elements later in this book.

A Perspective on Perspective

Globalization is shifting the tectonic plates of politics, economics, and sociology. Today, in order to lead with an authoritative voice, one must first understand the voices, hearts, and minds of those listening. One must have a firm estimate on the most likely response to a leader's words. In essence, one must possess a perspective on perspective.

This master perspective not only elongates influence in a localized sense, but creates a transportable, mobile chemistry that is invaluable, with immeasurable potential. The new cultural leader has the ability to spontaneously adjust, truncate, and revise language. This skill is cultivated on purpose. This cultivation is birthed out of an intentional desire to understand multiple cultures, long before the need to connect arises.

Transportable chemistry also refers to the ability to suspend personal feelings, biases, and premises in order to relate to the feelings, biases, and premises shared by followers. This chemistry mirrors, prioritizes, and communicates third-party concerns in a manner that elicits the response, "Hey, that's exactly what I've been thinking all along." Many leaders make the mistake of conjuring up new ideas without input from followers. People often don't appreciate new ideas being sprung upon them, their workplace, their processes; they need their own ideas expressed from a position of authority. Many of the answers for corporate, social, and even economic problems already exist in the common day-to-day thoughts of the average person. These thoughts simply have no voices, no literary artists to carefully refine their expression. This is why the plain-speaking, culturally relevant leader who captures and illuminates the common voice is influential beyond measure.

Effective communication—the kind of communication that assimilates to its environment like water—is the cornerstone of cultural leadership. Cultural leaders' communication style has little or no shape of its own, no preference but the preference that appeals to the broadest cultural base. This is a fundamental tenet of cultural leadership and does not refer to a cultivated skill, in a political sense, that simply pretends to be concerned or one that generates promises that expire one day after election. This is not "I'll say what you want to hear," but rather "I hear what you want to say."

To overcome the historically insincere facade practiced by outdated leadership theories is a real challenge. As a result, one must move slowly when establishing cultural leadership. This is not an overnight repositioning. Some of the most skeptical audiences are those on guard for cultural patronizing. Regardless of whether the audience is an HR department, a government office, or sports team, the rules are the same. Any culture can sense when a leader uses a term that is foreign to their everyday lexicon or references to a colloquialism they have simply never used. Facades don't establish cultural communication or transportable chemistry—in fact, they prevent it.

Hearts hear much better than ears. True cultural leadership understands what matters most to the heart of the culture: those long-held, uncompromising beliefs that can neither be bought nor sold. To locate and speak credibly to this sacred space is to establish a leadership that will be offered to you, one that is ultimately granted rather than taken.

A New Way of Thinking

How should leadership be defined? Before attempting to answer, one must be comfortable aiming at a moving target, because there is no single, agreed-upon definition. Add to this a dynamic global society with evolving needs and perspectives, and the leadership answer becomes rather ethereal. Military, political, religious, corporate, and social leadership can look very different, yet they all have certain common elements.

The key to uncovering these common elements is an understanding of what leadership is not. Leadership, in a global society, is no longer empty boldness or the ability to dress ugly opinions with beautiful rhetoric. In a global society, leadership is connection: a chemistry that begins, and is cultivated, at the grassroots level—but is not stuck there.

In their research paper "Social identity and the dynamics of leadership: Leaders and followers as collaborative agents in the transformation of social reality," Stephen Reicher (University of St Andrews), S. Alexander Haslam (University of Exeter) and Nick Hopkins (University of Dundee) present the following point: "Traditional models see leadership as a form of zero-sum game in which leader agency is achieved at the expense of follower agency and vice versa." They reject this notion, explaining, "Leadership is a vehicle for social-identity based collective agency in which leaders and followers are partners. There are two sides to this partnership: the way in which a shared sense of identity makes leadership possible and the way in which leaders act as entrepreneurs of identity in order to make particular forms of identity and their own leadership viable."

This premise that leaders should be viewed in part as entrepreneurs of identity is profoundly intuitive and invaluable to understanding the cultural leadership model. The word culture originates from the Latin *colere*, and is translated as "to build on, to cultivate, and to foster." Cultural leadership is, at least denotatively, a leadership that brings people together and builds upon differences in an effort to foster cooperation. Practicing outdated theories of leadership that are based on charisma and perception is over. A fatal dagger has been thrust into its philosophical heart. This in no way means that natural, inherent characteristics are irrelevant; they are not. It means only that sole dependence on these character traits is no longer effective.

Leadership is being redefined as the ability to become relevant. This relevance is defined by a leader's ability to listen and more effectively repeat ideas that are birthed from deep places of race, ethnicity, intelligence, and even ignorance. This is a fragile balancing act. There have been qualitative studies on which characteristics define a special, transformative leader. Most challenging is the fact that different cultures admire different traits. What works on Wall Street doesn't necessarily work in Tokyo, and what is viewed as strength in one culture is seen as weakness in another. This is a fragile balancing act. In the words of Robert J. House, director of the Global Leadership and Organizational Behavior Effectiveness Research Program at the Wharton School, "One size does not fit all." House spent over a decade studying and quantifying multicultural attributes of leadership. His conclusions make clear the need for today's leader to not only be well traveled and well learned, but also in control of his natural tendencies. By natural tendencies, I mean the bias to favor what has worked in the past in other situations and places. Cultural leaders must reflect the people they represent, not project their own opinions onto them.

Another perspective on leadership is the role of charisma, as it is increasingly received with caution, and for good reason. Charisma can be viewed in a couple of ways. One is an intangible aura that simply emanates from a leader. This aura can draw crowds and captivate in intimate settings as well as entire nations without having much substance to support the attention garnered. Another view is true charisma, which can have the same effect on the masses. The difference is, this influence is authenticated by true connections that have grown out of transportable chemistry.

Hitler was charismatic in the first order. In Hitler's case, arrogance, among other untamed characteristics nearly led to the extinction of the Jews. The atrocities he committed can at times prevent onlookers from learning how he was able to do it. He was one man. Surely he couldn't have killed millions of Jews alone— but his influence could. This is a vital point. Charisma is a field soldier that will do the bidding of a leader, even when the leader isn't present. Charisma is convincing and can lead millions to ignore logic and morality in an effort to submit to what they view as a higher intelligence that only their leader can access.

Hitler leveraged unreasonable arguments in the worst ways possible. He viewed himself as an artist who was singularly gifted with correctly painting the societal portrait. This is opposite to cultural leadership in every way. True cultural leadership replaces "them" with "we." Cultural leadership consolidates groups not by eliminating individuality, but rather by acknowledging and honoring it. This is where the GLOBE studies on how leadership, race, ethnicity, and expectation are profoundly intertwined. Let's look at how transportable chemistry created a cultural leader out of President George W. Bush.

.

Chapter 2

The Chemistry of Tragedy

Bush, Forty-third U.S. President: An Unlikely Cultural Leader

Cultural leadership runs on a narrow two-way street. That which establishes a leader as "one of the boys" may also work to send the same leader into philosophical exile, an exile where those who once most emphatically followed now lead a riot to end the reign. Some have compared the presidency of George W. Bush to a Shakespearean tragedy with victorious peaks neutralized by disappointing troughs.

To properly understand the Bush presidency, one must understand what came before it. In 1994, Georgia Representative Newt Gingrich led a peaceful political revolt based on social ethics, political conservatism, fiscal responsibility, and patriotism. The end result was that the Republican Party took control of both the House of Representatives and the Senate during midterm elections. This was the first time in forty years that the Republicans controlled both parts of Congress houses. In the same year, a young man with a familiar name, George W. Bush, was elected governor of the state of Texas. Five years later, when then-Governor Bush announced he would run for the U.S.

presidency, the conservative base was ecstatic. The legacy of his father aside, George W. Bush represented a relatively youthful Republican and was thought to have the ability to take full advantage of the Republican momentum started in 1994 during the Gingrich revolt.

Ultimately, George W. Bush won the U.S. presidency after an elongated Florida voting dispute. The U.S. Supreme Court ended the dispute in 2000, deciding in favor of Bush. "W" came into office under the banner of compassionate conservatism, a rather new philosophy that allowed conservatives to hold fast to fundamental fiscal and foreign policy and a commitment to domestic social concerns.

Still a Leader

Whether one agrees with the Bush presidency and its philosophies or not, one cannot deny his formidable leadership, which was due to the formidable constituency he led. This point should not be missed, because it hits at the core of cultural leadership. True cultural leaders do not gain such titles from being intellectually robust or even orally eloquent. Many observers make the mistake of concentrating on the public-speaking flaws or the perceived absentmindedness of George W. Bush. In reality, these things barely matter.

While most Americans prefer their leaders be great communicators with a firm grasp of academia, such abilities do not make a leader. On the contrary, cultural leaders are great because of the great commitment of their followers. Numbers matter, and, by definition, big numbers matter more. Millions of conservative Republicans found in Bush the perfect representation of big Texas swagger, small-town sensibility, and Bible-based beliefs. This was the mantle Bush took into the White House. His leadership was set. However, his performance as a leader was yet to be witnessed.

Good or Great?

Many have wondered whether it is more important to be a great leader with good advisors or a good leader with great advisors. This line of thinking usually comes from a certain perspective that says presidents are simply figureheads being controlled by a game of wealthy puppeteers. This may be partially true, for every political party must, in some way, bow to the financial forces that subsidized their campaign. The real question is whether a figurehead has the interpersonal grit needed to make life-and-death decisions without being told what he should believe. On September 11, 2001, President George W. Bush had the opportunity to answer this question.

The terrorist attacks on the morning of September 11 changed everything. Never before had the leader of the free world been placed in such a critically important, globally observable position. The existence of twenty-four-hour news and the Internet presented the forty-third U.S. president with an unprecedented task, the likes of which his predecessors had never seen.

One Country, One Culture, One Leader

The political and philosophical lines normally drawn to separate Americans from each other are the same lines that erect a fence of solidarity around all Americans when the country is attacked. President Bush had enormous cultural support after September 11. The culture was fundamentally American. I say *fundamentally* because we saw other countries rid themselves of their nationalist tendencies in order to back America in its fight against terrorism.

On 9/11, nothing else but the attacks mattered. Millions watched the towers fall, children weep, and that terrible look of despair on the faces of those seeking to find their loved ones. These images did more for the Bush presidency than a century of strategic political planning could ever do. He was the leader. His leadership in the days following 9/11 was so powerful because it was so authentic. There was no script and no set up; there were just raw emotions from a terribly tragic event. During this time, Bush had the opportunity to become the leader of a new global constituency, not based on race or creed, but upon freedom, the most valued tenet of humanity. Although this global leadership wasn't fully realized, at least not in the Bush presidency, we did witness another element of cultural leadership: inspiration.

The Power of Inspiration

True influence is best earned through inspiration. When a leader inspires, he can do little wrong. His analysis may be off, and his strategy may be outdated, but if the listener is inspired, little else matters. For Bush, this opportunity to inspire would quickly dissipate. It is nevertheless interesting how the very potential of getting something correct can provide months of patience. When people want to be inspired, even average actions can be viewed through the prism of greatness.

"I Can Hear You!"

On September 14, 2009, President Bush stood at Ground Zero in New York City among the thousands of rescue workers. With his arm around the shoulder of a firefighter, President Bush, in sincere and simple language, inspired the world. Television viewers could still see the smoldering buildings in the background and almost smell the melted steel. Speaking through a bullhorn, President Bush spoke of the shared loss of the American people.

President Bush: Thank you all. I want you all to know—it [bullhorn] can't go any louder—I want you all to know that America today—America today is on bended knee, in prayer for the people whose lives were lost here, for the workers who work here, for the families who mourn. The nation stands with the good people of New York City and New Jersey and Connecticut as we mourn the loss of thousands of our citizens.

Rescue worker: I can't hear you!

President Bush: I can hear you! I can hear you! The rest of the world hears you! And the people—and the people who knocked these buildings down will hear all of us soon!

Rescue workers (chanting): USA! USA! USA! USA! USA! USA! USA! USA!

President Bush: The nation—the nation sends its love and compassion—

Rescue worker: God bless America!

President Bush: —to everybody who is here. Thank you for your hard work. Thank you for makin' the nation proud, and may God bless America.

Rescue workers (chanting): USA! USA! USA! USA!

Author and commentator David McDowell put it best when explaining this power of this ground zero moment:

> The power of rhetoric is dramatically demonstrated ... as people immediately saw a charismatic quality in Bush that hadn't really been evident ... especially the moment when Bush touches the raw nerve of the crowd. At the moment he says "I can hear you," he seems to ignite patriotic passions in the hearts of the onlookers, kick-starting an outpouring of emotion. Seizing the moment, Bush repeats the phrase and then expands on it, rising to a climax as he vows revenge against the perpetrators. That sparks off a frenzy of baying from the crowd. Interestingly, someone in the crowd yells "God bless America!" and Bush quickly echoes it back to the crowd, signifying a two-way flow—a bond—between him and the crowd.

This is the best example of inspiration delivered to those in need of its power. Those cultural leaders with the sensitivity and ability to deliver this universally sought-after virtue are given influence far beyond that which they seek. It is the ability to encourage the heart to go that extra mile. Inspiration doesn't create; rather, it pushes over the edge that which already exists and gives air to timid wings that need just a bit of lift. This is the essence of its power. This unforgettable story is only a microcosm of the power of cultural leaders who connect. President Bush gave us a peek into the solidarity possible when leaders listen.

Now, let's take a few moments to study culture from the academic prism of the Wharton GLOBE studies.

What the GLOBE Studies Revealed

Impressions, chemistry, and opinions are established instantly—many times, without a person even saying a word. You've heard people say, "I just like him" or "He just seems like a leader." How and where does this instant likability originate? Is it race, ethnicity, demeanor, appearance? Is it all of the above? Most opinions are based on other opinions. Each individual has a reservoir of information gathered from the hands of family, friends, and cultural tendencies for future use.

Every issue from politics to religion is established within this opinion database. Add to this database social interactions, confirmation of what works in what environments, and opinions on what groups or races are safe and what neighborhoods to stay away from, and you have ready-made impressions for every conceivable situation. How quickly are these opinions generated and acted upon? Opinions are formed instantly, subconsciously. For example, have you ever been walking down the street and caught a glimpse of a person walking toward you? Did you cross to the other side or stay the course? Both decisions are based on everything from race, dress, demeanor, time of day, and that intangible thing called discernment. We all do it, whether we realize it or not. This can be applied to the elevator, the grocery line, and so on.

Leaders can suffer the same "man walking on the street" bias. So how can leaders best position themselves? This question is critical to an effort to establish leadership credibility outside one's philosophical home base. If the street one travels is where they grew up, there is little chance for misunderstanding, but if a leader plans to travel outside the home base, there is much work to be done. Global leadership is cultural leadership, the distinct ability to reach beyond your natural zone. This is the premise of the GLOBE studies on culture and leadership.

In the words of Robert J. House, the Wharton School and GLOBE Principal Investigator, "Being global is not just about where you do business." This view set the tone for his legendary studies, viewed as invaluable for their cultural conclusions. The GLOBE studies are the Manhattan project of culture and leadership. Professor House led 170 co-investigators in sixty-two countries. The studies spanned more than twenty years, collecting and organizing data from 17,300 middle managers in 951 organizations. This research created the most authoritative academic/social data regarding cultural leadership to date.

The GLOBE studies reveal in-depth conclusions on links between cultural practices and biases, and how these factors affect perspective on leadership. At the core of all conclusions is a desire to uncover transportable behaviors universally viewed as favorable. GLOBE helps to answer the question, "To what extent is leadership culturally defined?" The answers are very revealing.

Several approaches were used to make the GLOBE studies relevant. To avoid the force-fitting of preconceived notions, niche instruments of cultural measurement were developed. Members of the target culture were consulted; careful translation was done. The results were reviewed and appropriately applied to the function and practices of a specific culture.

This is important because communication, whether verbal or nonverbal, can take very different pathways to the same place.

Sentiment is also difficult to discern in cultures where privacy and saving face are virtues. GLOBE investigators took extreme care to assure interpretation was provided by members of the culture being studied to avoid curve fitting.

After studying sixty-two societies, GLOBE uncovered insightful, common dimensions of cross-cultural leadership. It is important to understand that cultural dimensions identified by GLOBE are classified in two ways: practices, or "as is," and values, or "should be." This distinction provides depth to conclusions as participants not only describe the state of cultural affairs, but also the vision for what they consider a perfect society. Some of the most fascinating of the GLOBE findings are the comparisons between the real and the ideal, the practice and the value.

Dimensions identified include:
Cultural Dimensions:

- Performance orientation, uncertainty avoidance, humane orientation
- Institutional collectivism, in-group collectivism, assertiveness, gender egalitarianism
- Future orientation and power distance

Culturally endorsed Leadership Theory Dimensions:

- Charismatic/value based, team oriented, self-protective, participative
- Humane oriented and autonomous

Primary Leadership Dimensions:

- Administratively competent, autocratic, autonomous, charismatic/visionary
- Charismatic/inspirational, charismatic/self-sacrificial, conflict inducer, decisive
- Diplomatic, face-saver, humane orientation, integrity, malevolent, modesty

- Non-participative, performance oriented, procedural, self-centered, status consciousness, team collaborative, and team integrator

The GLOBE studies reveal the true niche nature of transportable chemistry in the form of cultural leadership—that all leadership is, in many ways, culturally and geographically defined, but can be globally transferable. The extent to which a leader can honestly interrogate and modify his leadership biases and assumptions that shaped the foundation of his leadership can run parallel to his ability to reach a broader, more diverse leadership base—and yes, even to his becoming leader of the free world.

Public servants running for office have long known a certain lesson: the Ivy League pedigree, MBA, or PhD will not get you elected. There are too many examples of candidates with superior education receiving little to no support among the electorate. Many presidents, senators, congressmen, and C-level executives have all understood how powerful the intangible elements of persona and "that thing" can be. Although "that thing," which many people refer to in an effort to articulate a person's success without obvious reason, is difficult to teach, it is possible to trace "that thing" and learn from it.

Cultural Leadership and the White House

In 2008, Barack Obama won the presidential election—the first African American to be elected to the office. His election provides a profound insight into why cultural leadership is so vitally important, so powerful, and so relevant. Barack Obama is the finest contemporary example of a true cultural leader. Obama, in many ways, is the paragon of everything the GLOBE studies revealed years before anyone knew his name.

Obama conducted himself with controlled confidence, shrewd management, diplomacy, and a value-based charisma that he strategically displayed at will. He rejected highlighting elements of his background that elevated him above the common person. Although his origins were humble, he was neither common nor uneducated; quite the opposite. Many leaders miss one of the most important practices displayed by Obama: he allowed his elevation to come from the hands of others, never his own. This only fueled his intangible likability ratings, because in reality, no one could really trace where his rise was actually coming from. It is difficult to attack an invisible quality. He had "that thing."

Detractors who felt Obama didn't possess leadership skills to guide America into the future made one fatal mistake. Many of them continually asked the public on radio, television, and print one question, "Why are you voting for Obama?" Now, this seems rather innocent, until you read between the lines of the most common answer.

Most media outlets continually played respondents saying, "I don't know" or "We just need a change." For reasons we will discuss later in this book, Obama is a benchmark example for cultural leadership. To dismiss his win as a Democratic victory or Republican defeat is infinitely shortsighted. His win has nothing to do with political parties; it is all about relevance—and cultural relevance at its best.

When a leader has successfully tapped into the heart of a people, people support that leader from the deepest places of their being—so deep as to defy explanation. This is the reason many could not clearly articulate why they were voting for Obama. Ironically, this murkiness points to the clarity of his cultural leadership. In reality, there are very few words in our lexicon, no matter how learned we may be, that can adequately explain the reasons why we feel so deeply about certain people. Obama, for many, has become such a person.

Discerning Words, Discerning Actions

The GLOBE studies, as with all tenets of cultural leadership, revolve around an irreducible skill: communication.

Communication, verbal and nonverbal, is the wheels that transport the elegant dimensions of cultural leadership. Communication is more than the ability to speak and speak well. It is the ability to discern how and when to dial back the elegance of your ability to better fit certain situations. Relating to factory workers in Detroit takes an entirely different skill set than relating to bankers in New York. Both are two separate cultures requiring cultural communication.

Remember transportable chemistry? It travels by way of communication. Imagine you have been given a Bentley Azure, one of the finest, most expensive luxury vehicles. Hand-stitched leather seats, personal refrigerator, privacy windows—all customized at the desire of the consumer. Yet, it is the cheap part of the vehicle that is the most important: the tires. Without them, you have a stationary pile of expensive metal and leather. Communication transports chemistry. Communication can take you anywhere you want to go. It represents the most valuable tool of the cultural leader.

In the following chapters, I will delve deeper into all aspects of the GLOBE studies as they relate to transportable chemistry to establish cultural leadership. The world is bigger and smaller at the same time. The next chapter deals with this contradiction and how to harness its power.

Chapter 3

The Case for a New Model of Leadership

Continents Have Become Neighborhoods

There is no distance. The time it takes to reach across the world has been so truncated as to be nonexistent. Global collaboration that once took intercontinental flights now only requires Web cams and phone lines. This changes everything. Continents are now neighborhoods.

In the not-too-distant past, your neighborhood was the five or six blocks physically surrounding your house. The neighborhood was homogenous, with all the residents having at least one factor in common, be it an industry, a nationality, a lifestyle, socioeconomic status, or maybe just a desire to be outside of the hustle and bustle of the city. For many parents and grandparents, the world was aligned much differently.

The common beliefs and similar background of the neighborhood often led to shared values. There was little risk that a neighbor would be insulted or even upset when another corrected bad behavior in a teenager or watched for suspicious activity. No one thought twice about offering specific holiday-based greetings to their neighbors, and everyone celebrated similar ideas and ideals. The culture was essentially monolithic.

Then, rapidly, the world began to change and people had to adjust to a new type of neighborhood. As the world became more interconnected, people began to develop connections with neighbors quite different from themselves—and even connecting with others they had never met in person, but with whom they shared a common interest.

While the expansion began with the widespread adoption of the Internet as a communication device, the major methods of relating remained the same. People assimilated in groups that were much like themselves. They found people with shared interests and shared values. That's why the first successful online communities segregated people by interest groups.

Remember when America Online ruled the world? Everyone participating in the AOL service was encouraged to join user groups and discussion forums lists that revolved around a certain interest—a culture, if you will. People were not expected to connect with one another locally or internationally without a common interest, but they were expected to connect. At first, the goal was not to celebrate or even understand our inherent differences, but to minimize them and concentrate fully on similarities. We were told that the differences didn't matter, that we were all the same underneath our skin, that we had a common simplicity. The business world got involved, and people were expected to make connections with coworkers and clients with whom they, on the surface, had absolutely nothing in common. The one driving force in this new neighborhood was a shared work experience.

This new interactivity, now called globalization, happened so rapidly that many people didn't have a chance to fully understand their new, cross-cultural coworkers. E-mail, voice-over Internet protocols, instant messaging, and every imaginable electronic device made it easier to communicate with a coworker in Singapore than with your next-door neighbor. The world became larger, yet more intimate at the same time. Cultures were interacting, and globalization took flight.

What does globalization mean in general? What does it mean to you, specifically? There are no easy answers. Globalization immediately brings up tensions as people express concerns that a smaller, more interactive world might have a negative impact on their own success. Let's discuss how globalization came into its current form.

A Shrinking World Shrinks Biases

Until World War II and even for some time after it, many parts of the world were isolationist, concentrating only on doing what was best for the people within their borders. With the exception of major conflicts, much of what happened and what life was like in other parts of the world were ignored, misunderstood, or both.

Nations had a tendency to form alliances with other nations with similar values and world philosophies. In many ways, the world was like a global high school with groups forming based on perceptions, real or misconstrued, regarding other countries. For many, it was a geographic decision, with countries choosing to be closest, in terms of military and political alliances, to those with whom they were physically closest.

Another major factor tended to be history. Some countries tended to have a love-hate relationship with the First World nations, the old colonialists that helped found the younger nations. Though the British Empire had long since been divided, former British colonies maintained tight ties to the United Kingdom, most of Latin and South America maintained close ties to Spain, and so on.

But with the end of World War II came a new means of dealing with other countries diplomatically: the creation of the United Nations. With this creation, many countries began to interact more frequently and were forced to set aside prejudices and misconceptions that had ruled for years. The United Nations provided an international means for people to interact on universal issues. In the early stages, health issues like disease prevention and the spread of disease brought together humanitarians from every nation. Later, the Declaration of Human Rights, an internationally drafted and accepted document that claims human beings are born with certain rights regardless of their national origin, was introduced.

As interaction with the rest of the world made it harder to treat other people poorly based on the misinformation of the past, we entered the information age. First, television shared images from around the world. While the information might still have been skewed by what the source decided to show, there were visual images of the rest of the world. This forced many people to abandon their preconceived ideas. Travel between the nations became faster. Human connectivity advanced.

Today, the Internet has made it easy to make friends with people you have never seen or physically met. You may not even know their real names. This has led to relationships with people from different cultures in a very organic fashion. Stereotypes are increasingly dwindling. The fear of globalization has slipped away, and cultural relevance is now at the forefront. People want connection.

Realities and Misconceptions

In the minds of many, the term globalization had a negative connotation because it reflects cultural imperialism, the idea of conquering lesser developed nations via the export of culture, goods, services, and ideas, rather than military. To others, the concept of globalization meant going offshore with jobs and resources, depleting their nation's economic strengths through the leaching of good-paying jobs and the exporting of capital. The Globalization Website, created by sociology professors and others at Emory University to discuss the concept of globalization, defines it this way: "Globalization broadly refers to the expansion of global linkages, the organization of social life on a global scale, and the growth of a global consciousness, hence to the consolidation of world society" (Lechner 2001, 1).

The problem then is that most people do not view globalization through the eyes of the empirical scientist, but instead apply their own feelings and experience to it. Unemployed due to your job being outsourced? Then your thoughts are probably negative, as you view globalization as the cause of your economic woes. For a great many economists and political scientists, the process is also viewed negatively. "Among critics of capitalism and global inequality, globalization now has an especially pejorative ring" (Lechner 2001, 1). The problem is that economists and political scientists they equate globalization with exploitation, the concept of moving to or using resources from another country solely because of the ability to use that region's resources to replace resources that are used up or too expensive in their home region. In plain English, they equate globalization with slave labor, paying workers what can barely be considered a living wage because the people in that region are too poor to refuse.

However, all opinions are not necessarily the same. Nobel Prize–winning economist and Harvard University Professor of Economics Amartya Sen has written extensively on the concept of globalization and what it means to the less developed nations of the world and to the so-called First World nations.

> Throughout history, adventurers, generals, merchants, and financiers have constructed an ever-more-global economy. Today, unprecedented changes in communications, transportation, and computer technology have given the process new impetus. As globally mobile capital reorganizes business firms, it sweeps away regulation and undermines local and national politics. Globalization creates new markets and wealth, even as it causes widespread suffering, disorder, and unrest. It is both a source of repression and a

catalyst for global movements of social justice and emancipation. (Global Policy Forum 2008)

Sen has written extensively promoting the concept of globalization, if it is done in a manner that he considers appropriate. As an economist, Sen does not deny there is, at least initially, a hint of exploitation in the move to international business. Corporations would be ignorant not to take advantage of the resources. So, if the cost of labor in India is a fraction of what it is in Indiana, and you can achieve the same results, why not go to India?

> [I]t is hard to deny that there is some difficulty in persuading a great many people—making them "see" —that globalization is a manifest blessing for all, including the poorest. The existence of this confrontation does not make globalization a bad goal, but it requires us to examine the reasons for which there is difficulty in making everyone see that the globalization is manifestly and undoubtedly good. (Sen 2004)

In his speech at a United Nations conference on globalization, Sen argued that the important part of the globalization process was to let capitalism do its job and equalize the standard of living around the world. He further argued that capitalism might even be the path to the destruction of totalitarian regimes (2004).

Furthermore, he claims that we can already begin to see the effects of globalization as it begins to overcome the overwhelming poverty of some parts of the world. "The achievements of globalization are visibly impressive in many parts of the world. We can hardly fail to see that the global economy has brought prosperity to quite a few different areas on the globe. Pervasive poverty and 'nasty, brutish and short' lives dominated the world a few centuries ago, with only a few pockets of rare affluence" (Sen 2004).

Another challenge of globalization is the impact that it may have on the economies of so-called First World nations. In the United States, much of the rhetoric against the process of globalization stems from the loss of high-paying blue-collar jobs, which are being exported. Union leaders and others claim that the greed of businesses has destroyed the economy. Business owners can counter-argue that the greed of blue-collar workers made the transition necessary.

The simple truth about globalization is that it is not simple. Businesses must employ international trends to compete in the world market and yet still maintain some semblance of commitment to the local people for reasons of public relations. The coming years will make the debate much more severe as we try to address the worldwide recession that appears to be beginning.

To make the most of the available resources in a shrinking world, we must first understand the world as it is. The world is not a homogeneous entity. The world is a collective of people with different needs, different backgrounds, and different motivations.

The Changing Demographics of the World

This global world is not our parents' world. India and China both have more than a billion people, while the population is actually declining in many European nations. Even the concept of the nation is evolving, with the European Union replacing individual countries as the major regulatory overseer of France, Germany, Spain, and a swath of Western Europe. Thus, the way our parents related to even our closest allies has to change.

For centuries, until Richard Nixon opened China in the early 1970s, China was an unknown entity. In spite of the fact that China is the biggest country both in land mass and population in the world, it was, at best, a secondary player in the world market. A generation later, it has the world's largest economy and, as a consequence, is the world's biggest polluter. But despite China's enormous productivity, much of the nation remains in poverty.

China itself is a dichotomy caused by the rapidly evolving world, with world-wise cities along its coastlines and interior provinces struggling to eke out a living. It is also a microcosm of what is going on around the world. The infrastructure is insufficient to meet the needs of the populace and industry as well, straining the local regulators virtually to the breaking point.

With declining populations in Western Europe and population growth slowing among Caucasian groups in the United States, the face of business is changing as well. The days of old white men in suits running the world are long gone. Businesses must adjust to the concept of a much more diversified population in the workforce and at the helm of important multinational corporations.

The problem then arises when these diverse groups all arrive with their own prejudices and misconceptions about one another. Historically, Christians and Muslims have fought countless battles, but now we find that people of both faiths and dozens of others are being asked to work side by side. Shared memories, from Christmas parties to Independence Day picnics, are less commonly held, and in many cases don't exist. Even the generational gap is growing; today's young adults have never known a world without the interconnectivity of the Internet and the immediate access to information it provides.

To adjust to the changing demographics of the world, we must first understand them. To assume anything about a person's religious beliefs, based on their country of origin, race, or even mode of dress is something we must avoid in our new interactive, multicultural world.

Complex Adaptive Systems / Spontaneous Assimilation

Change is the only constant. The rapid expansion of emerging markets, continued volatility in commodity prices, technological advances, and increasing consumer sophistication are just some of the factors that can result in abrupt shifts in global markets for goods and services. Indeed, any one of these factors can have dramatic effects on business performance. If companies, managers, and leaders are to survive, they must find new ways to adapt quickly to ever-changing conditions.

Traditional approaches involving continuous improvements in the top-down control and direction of organizations simply are not flexible enough to keep pace with dynamic markets. Successful companies are moving to organic, self-organizing models that focus on creating the conditions for more autonomous internal agents and processes to naturally find order in the midst of chaos. These new business models are called complex adaptive systems.

In "Seven Layers for Guiding the Evolving Enterprise," Philip Anderson describes the benefits of complex adaptive systems, noting, "In natural systems order emerges as long as a system has an inflow of energy, enough parts, enough interconnections, and positive feedback loops.... Such systems tend to evolve to a state between inertia and chaos called 'self-organization' or 'the edge of chaos.'

Anderson notes that over recent decades, most major companies have pursued knowledge management approaches and other techniques to enhance their ability to respond in real time to changing circumstances. Nevertheless, these techniques have not achieved the spontaneous assimilation needed to keep pace with, much less profit from, quickly changing developments in our turbulent world economy. The next evolution for so-called learning organizations is movement toward complex adaptive systems. According to John H. Holland (1998), a complex adaptive system can be defined as

> A dynamic network of many agents (which may represent cells, species, individuals, firms, nations) acting in parallel, constantly acting and reacting to what the other agents are doing. The

> control of a [complex adaptive system] tends to be
> highly dispersed and decentralized. If there is to
> be any coherent behavior in the system, it has to
> arise from competition and cooperation among the
> agents themselves. The overall behavior of the
> system is the result of a huge number of decisions
> made every moment by many individual agents.

The term complex adaptive system was taken from the natural sciences. In nature, evolution takes place through a continuous cycle of experimentation that drives genetic processes. These experiments may seem random, involving changes in the size, shape, color, and mating behaviors of animals and other organisms. Nevertheless, they ultimately determine which species survive and which become extinct. The organisms gifted with favorable variation live longer, reproduce more, out-compete others, and ultimately dominate future generations (Pietersen 2002).

The challenge for leaders is to strike a fine balance between providing direction for the overall company and encouraging autonomy among independent agents. In a cross-cultural context, this is particularly difficult, as individual managers must act within a combination of international norms and local expectations derived from values and beliefs held within particular work environments. In short, they must communicate with, and cater to the needs of, large groups that are often both geographically and culturally diverse in order to drive and steer movement for the system as a whole.

As Anderson (1999) observes, complex adaptive systems have three main attributes: variation, selection, and retention. Using the example of a giraffe, he explains that the process of evolution began with variation, when a few giraffes were born with necks that were longer than average. The selection process was based on the fact that these giraffes could reach some sources of food that others could not access. Thus, these giraffes found it easier than others to flourish and breed. Retention is the process by which the giraffes with longer necks were able to pass their genes onto their children. Over time, the population of long-necked giraffes was able to out-maneuver and outperform other members of the species that had shorter necks and thus less access to nourishment.

Companies that serve as market leaders will necessarily encompass the processes and communication networks needed to encourage and reward experimentation. These organizations will actively seek not only continuous improvement in current business processes, but also entirely new approaches that help them adapt to, and occasionally alter, the current business environment.

Increasingly, the thinking on complex adaptive systems is making its way into the business world, as more companies recognize that continual adaptation and renewal are critical to stay afloat in the midst of ever-shifting markets. The leaders of tomorrow recognize today's business environment is complex, comprising a multitude of interconnected elements that are often disbursed across countries and cultures. Let's look at a few corporate examples.

Chapter 4

Corporate Chemistry

Adaptation

One example of a company that has moved to a more complex adaptive system is Capital One Financial Corporation. Headquartered in McLean, VA, this financial holding company with 725 locations throughout the United States was ranked second in North America and fifth globally on *Fortune* magazine's 2007 list of Global Top Companies for Leaders.

Capital One's approach can be likened to the system of evolution found in nature. First, it is engaged in a cycle of continuous experimentation, introducing some one hundred fifty thousand pilots for new products each year. These pilots are carried out at low cost, and only 1 percent is taken forward based on early market feedback. This early testing and feedback system enables Capital One to quickly predict the likely value consumers will attach to prospective new products before engaging in costly roll-out procedures. Second, workers at Capital One are seen as semiautonomous; it is everyone's job to take the initiative to work outside traditional boundaries when the need to do so arises. Finally, when Capital One's experimentation identifies a new product as a potential winner, the company deploys it quickly and with a force that positions the new product as an early leader within its given market niche before competitors catch on, much less catch up (Anderson 1999).

So, what is needed to make the successful transition to complex adaptive systems? Companies must change the way they view organizational structure and leadership in order to create systems of spontaneous assimilation. Often this entails letting go of perceptions held in the past. The leading companies and managers no longer come from North America and Europe, and they have expanded their communications and operational networks far beyond the bounds of those regions.

The development of air cargo services illustrates that many new companies are literally global networks. Over the past two decades, overnight deliveries have grown to represent more than 50 percent of the delivery market in the United States, and they are projected to represent more than 30 percent of the world market by the end of the next decade. This market is dominated by a few major companies that are less than thirty years old and literally operate on a spoke network, where shipments within a country are picked up and delivered to a central hub. They are then bundled and redirected to points across the globe.

For example, Federal Express (FedEx) operates major hubs across 130 different countries from a key network site in Memphis, TN, and a newly established central hub in southern China. Over the past three years, FedEx's revenue has grown by more than 20 percent to exceed $35 billion a year.

As the air delivery market continues to expand in line with the growth of the world economy, these companies involved will necessarily continue to expand and diversify their workforces. Employment in the industry was over half a million workers in 2002.

Global expansion almost always means cultural expansion. In 2007, *Black Enterprise* magazine named FedEx one of the 40 Best Companies for Diversity. FedEx has consistently outperformed its peers in terms of the percentage of African Americans and other minorities represented in the workforce, senior management positions, and the board of directors. It also devotes a high percentage of total procurement dollars to suppliers owned by African Americans and members of other minority groups. FedEx has been named among the Best Places to Work in more than twenty different countries. In 2008, it made *Fortune* magazine's list of 100 Best Companies to Work For.

According to Judy Edge, Corporate Vice President of Human Resources, "FedEx values and promotes the unique contributions, perspectives, and differences of our team members worldwide." Frederick W. Smith, chairman, president, and chief executive officer, stresses the important role of the workplace in providing outstanding service to customers. In a 2008 interview with *Fortune* magazine, he said:

> The FedEx culture, centered on our people-first philosophy, has always been a major competitive advantage. Motivated, committed team members providing the highest possible service levels are what separate us from the competition. Putting people first makes very good business sense and is the right thing to do. (*Fortune* 2008)

Structure

In contrast to traditional hierarchical structures with firm boundaries separating departments, divisions, and so forth, complex adaptive systems focus on the need for self-organization, knowledge, and continuous feedback loops in order to ensure long-term survival.

Everyone in the organization is charged with moving outside traditional roles and organizational boundaries should the need to do so arise. At the same time, positive and negative feedback drives and reinforces the need to adjust inputs and outputs. Many of these enterprises lack rigid rules and planning mechanisms. Instead, changes emerge in response to evolving complex interdependencies. Just as we may don or shed a jacket as changes occur in the weather, successful companies build on their ability to adjust to changing market conditions. Finally, successful organizations carefully take into account small changes in their internal and external environments, or so-called butterfly effects. Even minor changes in interest rates, government regulations, or commodity prices can significantly alter market trends and expectations.

Leadership

The rigid, hierarchical organizational structures of the past relied on managers to put in place policies, work practices, and rules to be followed in pursuit of stated business goals. In today's complex environment, many companies are taking advantage of a diverse global workforce that is often dispersed geographically across countries and regions. For example, it is not at all uncommon for a project manager in the United States to work in a virtual capacity, with a design team located in Japan and procurement professionals in Mexico to oversee a project in China. Thus, today's work environment comprises a larger number of separate, individual, intelligent agents that are empowered to make decisions aimed at achieving certain goals. This environment naturally calls for a shift from management to cultural leadership.

The GLOBE studies define leadership as "the ability of an individual to influence, motivate, and enable others to contribute toward the effectiveness and success of the organizations of which they are members." The studies also found that some specific leadership behaviors are universally endorsed across cultures, while others may be seen as culture-specific.

Effective leadership requires that an individual has both universal leadership traits and those traits valued as important in the culture where he must operate. As discussed above, the cross-cultural dimensions required for effective leadership regardless of culture include trust, empathy, transformation, power, and communication.

I would add the need for effective conflict management skills to the list. The speed at which business takes place in today's world of continual connections (via the Internet and cell phones) leaves little time for individuals to reflect, consider, and think.

Ironically, there is also less time for purposeful communication and more room for misinformation, ambiguity, and misunderstanding. This makes it imperative that leaders effectively communicate the mission and direction for action; ensure team members are given the time needed for positive interaction within the system; and mediate misunderstandings, including those with cross-cultural roots. In this respect, leaders must build the bridge between cultural diversity and repeatable business processes within an increasingly competitive business environment. Let's look at real world examples.

Transformational Leadership 3.0

In the book *The World Is Flat: A Brief History of the Twenty-first Century* (2006), Thomas L. Friedman describes the changes occurring in international markets and businesses as what he calls Globalization 3.0. He argues that through globalization, the world is shrinking and diverse groups are becoming empowered as part of the business mainstream. These changes, which have brought about remote work, distributed operations, and changing organizational structures, have added new dimensions to traditional leadership models as businesses and other organizations adjust the ways in which work is designed and performed.

Over the past two decades, transformational leadership has been the key paradigm undergirding most leadership theories (Beyer 1999). Transformational leaders are distinct because they provide inspirational motivation and intellectual stimulation and treat followers with individual consideration (Bass & Avolio

1994). In essence, they transform their followers' needs, values, and preferences in order to generate higher levels of performance around shared goals (Seltzer & Bass 1990).

As James Burns explains in *Leadership* (1978), this type of leadership changes both leaders and followers as groups engage with one another to increase levels of motivation and performance. Thus, leadership effectiveness depends not so much on individual behavior, but on collaborative processes.

Unlike the command-and-control systems of the past, organizational structures are perceived as networks of individuals across a variety of levels sustained by social interactions and networks of influence. Friedman suggests that increased globalization is adding important new dimensions to the transformational leadership model that call for ever greater collaboration. It also calls on the model to take into account greater cultural and social diversity and different assumptions concerning geographical space and time. The findings of 2007 Center for Creative Leadership (CCL) survey on leadership skills support Friedman's analysis. Its focus on how Globalization 3.0 has affected the ways corporate executives around the world view leadership in the current environment confirms that leaders' ability to collaborate effectively across business units and cultures will be critical in the period ahead.

While the survey shows that leaders in Asia and Europe have already begun to embrace more collaborative styles of leadership, most U.S. companies still adhere to traditional, command-and-control approaches. Nevertheless, the adjustment of leadership style is fast becoming mandatory.

Power Sharing

In a recent interview with *Fast Company* magazine (2008), John Chambers, chairman and CEO of the IT giant Cisco Systems, explains how his company was forced to rethink its operations in the wake of the IT sector crisis. Suddenly faced with more than

$2 billion in write-downs and eight thousand layoffs, Cisco was able to find the solutions it needed through collaboration. According to Chambers, the company, which had once relied on only ten top executives to make decisions, now includes more than five hundred individuals in strategic planning. While decisions on promotions and compensation were once made based on individual performance, they are now determined by collective business goals. Moreover, innovation in the company—once dependent on the distribution of power among competitors is now open to a range of boards and councils representing the entire spectrum of stakeholders. As a result of this shift toward collaborative leadership, Chambers says, the company has managed to get its profits up and operating expenses down.

Although there is no clear consensus on a blueprint for leadership in the Globalization 3.0 era, the CCL survey supports the experience of Cisco Systems. More important, it clearly shows that the ways that international businesses think about leadership are changing as companies search for new solutions. These challenges are strongly related to the increased diversity of the workforce and the growing geographical distribution of work units and individuals around the globe.

In response to questions about the primary challenges their organizations currently face, a majority of respondents to the CCL survey identified talent acquisition and development as high priorities. In the period ahead, respondents said their organizations will focus on collaborative leadership, in particular the ability to build effective teams, influence without authority, and foster change management. Thus, the most successful managers and organizations of the future will hone their networking skills in ways that enable them to tap into existing organizational cultures and power structures in order to collaborate more effectively. This means bringing together diverse individuals and business units scattered across geographical and functional areas in pursuit of common goals.

Cultural Dimension

Over the past two decades, much of the scholarship on leadership has placed emphasis on communicating across cultures. Indeed, leading cross-cultural groups has taken center stage within some circles, owing to the expansion of multinational operations and the outsourcing of manufacturing and business processes. Clearly, these changes in business processes call for leaders to develop cross-cultural awareness and the networking skills needed to take advantage of synergies among geographically dispersed business units. What has been less obvious to some is the need for cultural leadership within national organizational structures. The widespread mobility of the global workforce has literally changed the face of business domestically as well as internationally. Indeed, the past decade has been characterized by unprecedented cross-national migration. The United States, Canada, and Australia have welcomed the largest numbers of immigrants in history. During the 1990s, the U.S. immigrant population grew by 11.3 million; Canada's grew by nearly 500,000; and Australia's reached a fifteen-year high of 123,450 in 2005 (Camarota and McArdle 2003). Owing to the expansion of the European Union, the collapse of the former Soviet Union, and the economic boom in Asia, labor mobility and immigration has also reached an all-time high in Europe and China.

The increased diversity of national labor forces has made organizational culture more complex, as social and cultural generalizations have lost validity. Even within a domestic economy, such generalizations can be seriously misleading. For example, although the United States is a single country, it would be a mistake to assume that natives of New York City will share the same values and priorities as those living in rural Mississippi. Similarly, members of the highest caste in India are different from members of the lowest caste (McFarlin and Sweeney 2000). Moreover, personal cultural values are affected by a wide array of non-geographical factors, such as age, level of education, socioeconomic status, religion, and so on (Taras and Steel 2005).

Spatial Dimension

In today's business environment, the dimensions of time and space have taken on increased importance. Under the traditional organizational structures of the past, employees worked together, usually in the same building and for the same hours. Today, coworkers often collaborate and coordinate work activities across geographically dispersed locations. Because leaders often do not have the luxury of bringing people together physically, they have to adjust work processes to take into account different time zones and rely on emotional connections to rally people together around organizational missions, visions, and goals.

A recent study by Hermenia Ibarra and Mark Hunter (2007) finds that although physical separation and communication channels may be what the news media and organizations tend to focus on, the real driver in leadership effectiveness is the degree of psychological distance between leaders and followers. This psychological distance can be smaller in organizational structures that span national boundaries than in some companies that house all of their workforces in single buildings. The authors conclude:

> Regardless of where people are working, leaders need to make the time and take the effort to create personal connections with followers. This does not mean "playing favorites," but it does mean showing an interest by finding out what kinds of strengths individual employees have and then giving them opportunities to use those strengths. Although many leaders may not be used to having conversations with employees that go beyond the boundaries of the task at hand, rising to the challenge of making a personal connection can have dramatic results. Something as simple as sending a follow-up e-mail, praising an employee for a job well done, or asking an employee's opinion on a pending decision, can tighten bonds.

Followers will work harder, perform better, and be more satisfied with their jobs (Ibarra and Hunter 2007).

Change Networking

Thus, in the Globalization 3.0 business world, networking has taken on greater importance than ever before. It provides the foundation for collaborative leadership. It creates the fabric of personal contacts across business units, consumer groups, investors, and other stakeholders who provide support, feedback, insight, resources, and information. Nevertheless, many new leaders see networking as one of the most dreaded developmental challenges. As Ibarra and Hunter (2007) point out, the discomfort about networking experienced by many aspiring leaders is understandable. Networking is hard work. Moreover, while managers tend to move up corporate ladders based on their technical expertise and ability to achieve specific organizational goals, networking is about developing relationships across a broad and diverse range of individuals and groups. Networking is taking on increased importance in transformational and collaborative leadership. Thus, those who fail to make the switch in thought processes and priorities or those who discount this work as too political ultimately will fail. Either they will not be selected into leadership positions or they will falter once they attain them.

There are three distinct but interdependent types of networking:

- Operational
- Personal
- Strategic

The following section briefly discusses each of these forms of networking in turn, but the key to effective networking is the ability to leverage the elements from each domain into the others, seeking out and building personal relationships with strategic counselors, individual colleagues, and business units in order to form constituencies of support.

Operational Networking

Operational networking is focused on ensuring coordination and cooperation among individuals and groups who have to work together and trust each other in order to accomplish immediate tasks. These networks include not only direct superiors and subordinates within discrete business units, but also key players in associated units as well as suppliers, distributors, customers, and others. While the number and diversity of people involved in such networks can often be remarkable, the extent of membership is usually straightforward: either an individual's contribution is necessary to the task at hand or it is not. Still, the quality of working relationships, the personal rapport, and mutual trust within these networks give them their power.

Personal Networking

Personal networks include memberships in professional associations, alumni groups, clubs, and personal interest communities. These networks can be used effectively to further personal and professional development, advance career goals, and provide a foundation for strategic networking. Although these networks exist largely outside the walls of corporations, many successful leaders use them as venues to seek advice and insight on specific problems. Indeed, what makes personal networks powerful is the ability of members to exchange knowledge, advice, and referrals.

Strategic Networking

Strategic networking concerns ways to establish both vertical and lateral relationships across an organization, including among functional and business unit leaders, as well as a broad range of stakeholders, in order to address broad strategic issues. These networks include many members who are outside of the leader's immediate authority or control. Nevertheless, they represent a broad set of relationships and information sources the leader can draw on collectively to establish the coalitions needed to attain resources and sell ideas.

As Ibarra and Hunter (2007) observe:

> The key to a good strategic network is leverage: the ability to marshal information, support, and resources from one sector of a network to achieve results in another. Strategic networkers use indirect influence, convincing one person in the network to get someone else, who is not in the network, to take a needed action. Moreover, strategic networkers don't just influence their relational environment; they shape it in their own image by moving and hiring subordinates, changing suppliers and sources of financing, lobbying to place allies in peer positions, and even restructuring their boards to create networks favorable to their business goals.

Social Networking

Effective networking is difficult, precisely because it does take a significant amount of time and energy. For this reason, most successful leaders combine and leverage their efforts across all three of the dimensions discussed above. Some, like Gabriel Chenard, a general manager for a group of consumer products, use an inside-out approach. As Ibarra and Hunter (2007) describe, Chenard takes advantage of every site visit to build his network of relationships with employees and customers. Other successful leaders take an outside-in approach, using communities of practice in their areas of expertise to multiply their knowledge base and solidify connections within their industries.

Increasingly savvy leaders are tuning into the information revolution by using the Internet for social networking purposes. The Web provides numerous channels to build communities of practice both within individual companies and across entire industries in every area of business. At the time of this writing, the most used social networking sites on the Internet include Facebook, Twitter, and LinkedIn. LinkedIn is probably the most popular among business executives, with over 39 million members, including executives from all of the U.S. Fortune 500 companies, in over two hundred countries and territories around the world. As organizations move to networked structures, owing to joint ventures, alliances, and outsourcing operations, many companies are making greater use of social networking as a means of organizing work and promoting cooperation. For example, according to CIO Tim Schaefer, Facebook and LinkedIn are increasingly becoming part of Northeastern Mutual Financial Network's business. The company promotes the use of these sites for collaboration across business units and provides guidelines to help employees comply with company policies for posting information online (Stitt 2008). Schaefer notes, however, the Internet does not change relationship-based networking; it merely provides a new channel for it.

Against this background, it is still important for leaders to access informal networks within their organizations in order to facilitate collaboration among strategically important groups. While social networking sites provide an efficient channel for communication among top leaders, individual business units, and new product development teams, it is still important to nurture social relationships of trust and a common identity among these groups.

Anecdotal Success

In *The Tipping Point: How Little Things Can Make a Big Difference* (2000), Malcolm Gladwell identifies three types of social
networkers: Mavens, Connectors, and Salesmen. Mavens love to gather and share knowledge. Connectors are very social and seem to know everyone. They pass information along wherever it needs to go. Finally, salesmen are extremely persuasive. Their positive attitudes and ideas tend to be contagious. When these three types of people begin to interact within a social network, it is possible for leaders to accomplish specific goals or create big changes with astonishing speed.

A similar study by Karen Stephenson (2006) examines how information flows through social networks. She finds participants tend to fall into three archetypes: so-called hubs, gatekeepers, and pulse takers. Hubs are people who know many others within the group and thus are privy to a great deal of information. While hubs share their knowledge readily, they are not necessarily discerning in directing flows of information appropriately. Thus, it is not wise to share secrets with them. Gatekeepers, on the other hand, are experts in managing information, easily identifying with whom to share what and when. For this reason, gatekeepers are extremely valuable in building effective social networks. Pulse takers are also extremely valuable resources. Although they are usually active participants in a variety of networks, they often choose to avoid drawing attention to themselves. Instead, they prefer to observe the people, issues, and trends among groups. For this reason, pulse takers are excellent coaches, mentors, and agents for change.

In describing these three archetypes, Stephenson notes that one rarely meets a person who is a pure archetype. Rather, individuals tend to have characteristics of one or more of these types. Moreover, a few people, whom she calls strange attractors, may serve all three roles simultaneously. Although these people are rare, they can be powerful forces within organizations.

Therefore, she says, "They should be sparingly sprinkled into any recipe for change" (2006).

Whether developed through social networking sites on the Internet or within the confines of organizations, social networks can ultimately save or annihilate a company. Therefore, it is important for leaders to look beyond traditional or formal hierarchies to analyze the webs of social connections that exist within and around their organizations. These webs actually control the flows of information, knowledge, and power that comprise the work environment.

Social network insight is critical, especially within diverse and geographically dispersed work groups, to establishing the culture of trust needed to pull disparate business units together in ways that inspire innovation, information sharing, and confidence.

Spontaneous Assimilation

The word adaptive implies that companies must continually study the business environment and remain vigilant to emerging threats and opportunities. They must keep their internal operations highly connected in order to pull together the expertise needed to solve problems or take advantage of opportunities immediately as they arise. This is precisely what will enable them to survive and compete in an ever-shifting business world.

Nearly every market encompasses three variables— participants, market forces, and behaviors—which can signal impending change. It is imperative for leaders today to have an in-depth understanding of the key participants found at each level of the business chain, including customers, competitors, distributors, and suppliers, and the relationships and interactions that occur among them. This understanding is crucial to predict not only emerging customer needs and desires, but also the way in which key players may influence and shape other forces in the system that can have significant impacts on the environment as a whole. Such an understanding can inform the strategic formulation, design, and implementation of business processes while highlighting opportunities for both internal and external innovation and identifying the need for risk-management solutions. Continuous analysis of participants, forces, and behaviors entails staying abreast of:

- all participants involved in the market
- the relationships and interactions that exist among participants
- whether, and which, participants are entering or existing the market
- forces that affect all participants
- forces that affect particular participants or groups of participants
- behaviors that are predominant among participants
- behaviors that may be new or emerging

By understanding the nature of behaviors, influencing forces, and the relationships among participants in a system, leaders can develop the early detection systems needed to inform strategy, enable innovation, and identify threats for risk-management purposes. The ongoing shakeout of winners and losers in the global marketplace suggests that the leading companies of the twenty-first century will encompass complex adaptive systems where continuous experimentation is embraced as the key to survival. These companies will be characterized by internal cultures that maximize the opportunity for creativity and innovation. The business leaders of tomorrow will be ever vigilant to emerging changes in the specific environments in which they operate. They will effectively communicate direction while providing the individual worker is ensured of competency and freedom of decision making needed to achieve spontaneous assimilation. How quickly must leaders engage an adapting world? Now! I call it *Instant Intelligence.*

Chapter 5

Instant Intelligence

Cliff Notes Leadership

The moment something happens, the whole world knows about it. In a world of instant communication, leaders must create, maintain, and protect their public images. While an increasing number of experts are recognizing the importance of reputation risk management, there is little agreement on how best to do so. Experts do agree that today's leaders are faced with a world that is very different than the leaders of yesterday's world. Prior to the 1990s, electronic computers were large, expensive devises limited to large universities, corporations, and government agencies. People thought of the media in terms of a few highly influential broadcast networks and locally or nationally distributed newspapers or magazines (Branam 2003). In that era, external communication in the corporate world generally referred to small groups of ad men, who served as liaisons with media outlets and government agencies. That was then.

Current technological advances have changed lifestyles, spawned new industries, and focused entire populations around personal computers. As of 2008, more than 71.3 percent of the North American population used the Internet, up 127.9 percent from 2007. Worldwide, the increase of Internet usage was a staggering 290 percent (Internet Usage Statistics 2008). Today, people from all walks of life and all cultures flock to online sources for education, research, news, shopping, and entertainment. The development of increasingly user-friendly interfaces and ease of access afforded by high-speed networks is projected to further increase Internet usage, bridging the digital divide.

How does this affect leadership? People tend to accept whatever they see and hear at face value. Whether it is the character of a nation's leader, the value of a product or service, the integrity of a multinational corporation, or even the guilt or innocence of a person accused of an ethical violation, the media has an amazing influence on the public perception (Branam 2003). Leaders who ignore the age of instant intelligence make a terrible misstep. A leaders' ability to control his image has never been more vital than it is today.

Perhaps most challenging is the need for risk management in the area of communications. As the 2005 remake of the movie comedy *Fun with Dick and Jane* illustrates, millions can be won or lost on the spin of a thirty-second sound bite. Based on the Enron debacle, the premise for this film begins the day Globodyne's stock tanks and its pension fund evaporates. The corporate CEO and CFO set up an unsuspecting middle manager to serve as the public face of the company on live television moments before the disaster occurs. In today's age of instantaneous information, any manager could face the same dilemma as the movie character Dick Harper, as there is no longer time to spin new information. In this environment, leaders must think, and think again, before they speak. Words mean everything. They can mark the difference between minimizing damage and furthering disaster. While some may feel that leaders of companies that find themselves in situations like Globodyne's get what they deserve, it is clear that the information age of the twenty-first century has changed the communication rules of the game for everybody. Leaders must present clear, well targeted messages in a way that reduces the likelihood of distortion.

Internal Considerations

Reputation will guide the way your organization is perceived by the world. Usually, this is a reflection of its own internal culture and leadership. It is useless to pull together a marketing image you think will be attractive for investors and customers and just put it out there. That is not only bad governance, but also poor risk management. If your company—and its leadership—does not deliver on the promises made through the public relations campaign, it will be found out and lose trust, both within the company and among external observers.

One of the most important considerations, especially in a knowledge-based organization, is employee needs, which are not only economic, but also social and psychological. The leadership's ability to meet these needs in a transparent way will have significant influence on its ability to project a favorable image as a market leader. Again, projecting the ability to spontaneously adapt to market conditions and customer needs is critical. However, this is also one of the greatest challenges for corporate communications.

For many workers, including managers at all levels, change can be seen as disruptive or even threatening. But a corporate culture that values continuous effort to improve through change or reinforcing those processes that work is reinforced by a culture of learning. As employees learn, the collective organizational knowledge base grows. In such environments, change is less likely to be seen as disruptive and more likely to be welcome as an outcome of employee learning. This culture must be established based on trust. Employees need to understand why change is occurring, and they need to be incorporated into the change process. Anyone who feels excluded is more likely to negatively judge senior leaders and make efforts, including through the use of purposeful leaks, to hinder change.

Even brilliant management decisions that clearly bolster the potential success of the organization may be undermined by employees who distrust the change process or the company's leadership. This can be a particular problem in organizations with strong corporate cultures that are deeply embedded with traditions and values that have guided behavior over time. These cultures generally do not support the momentum needed to face ongoing and overlapping change. Indeed, many senior leaders may even view it is in their own interest to resist change, especially if it could negatively affect their personal positions or status.

External considerations

Along with internal forces, broad external conditions and societal trends also influence an organization's reputation. Significant external factors include the organization's ability to keep pace with technological and business advances as well as its capacity to adapt to economic, legal, political, social, and cultural norms. Therefore, leaders must thoughtfully establish and nourish a corporate culture that integrates continuous monitoring of the external environment with mainstream strategic and operational activities.

Changes in the external environment may serve as important clues or signals about where the organization is headed, not only in terms of its competitive position, but also in terms of its reputation among key stakeholders and the public at large. Therefore, leaders must be vigilant to even small changes in the business environment and analyze what they perceive realistically and intelligently in order to adapt quickly. In today's world of rapid information flows, it will be just as difficult to keep internal secrets or to spin bad news as it will be to prevent leaks. Therefore, it is imperative that leaders prepare frontline managers, employees, and other stakeholders for changes as they emerge.

Why Leaders Fail

Leaders by nature are risk takers. It is risky to assume you can lead others in a substantive fashion, expect your ideas can transform an organization, and lead others to share in a compelling cause. This naturally paints a rather obvious target on the philosophical chest of every leader. This is why leaders must be solid, not easily flustered. Confidence is paramount and the ability to process constructive criticism is vital. It should come as no surprise that risk takers experience failure, even the most capable leaders. It's part of the territory.

For example, most people see former U.S. Secretary of State Colin Powell as a great military leader. His reputation from the First Gulf War was stellar, and his intelligence, management savvy, and leadership style are beyond dispute. Yet he was not able to succeed within the administration of former U.S. President George W. Bush. This failure left many people in the United States and elsewhere wondering, "How can this be?" The answer is simple: culture.

The competition for the president's ear between the U.S. National Security Advisor and the U.S. Secretary of State is a constant topic of insider gossip in every U.S. presidential administration. National Security Adviser Condoleezza Rice became not only one of George W. Bush's top aides, but also a personal friend and confidant who regularly visited with the Bush family. According to Rice, this connection was based on a shared worldview and devout Christian values (Whitelaw et al. 2004). Meanwhile, Colin Powell approached his role as Secretary of State like a soldier, serving the Commander in Chief. As Whitelaw et al. (2004) point out, although Powell clashed repeatedly with Vice President Dick Cheney and Defense Secretary Donald Rumsfeld, most notably over Iraq, his general approach was to stand behind President Bush whether he agreed or not. According to his close advisors, Powell did help persuade Bush to seek the support of the United Nations in the U.S. conflict with Iraq. However, he saw his presentation before the U.N. General Assembly outlining the case on Iraqi weapons of mass destruction as the lowest point of his career, especially after finding out that U.S. intelligence was regarding the presence of such weapons (Whitelaw et al. 2004).

Even the strongest leaders sometimes fail when they find themselves in new positions and new organizational cultures that fall outside their comfort zones. Frequently, they face very high expectations to hit the ground running, developing a strong network of partners and followers and visibly helping their companies achieve great things. As a matter of fact, the failure rate among leaders is staggering. In the book *The First 90 Days: Critical Success Strategies for New Leaders at All Levels*, Michael Watkins reports that 58 percent of executives entering positions in new companies fail within the first two years. In 2007, U.S. companies experienced a turnover of 28,058 executives, including board members, CEOs, presidents, and vice presidents. This represents a 68 percent increase in turnovers since 2005 (Liberum 2007). The estimated cost to the organizations concerned is more than $1 million per failure! This places a different perspective on leaders who succeed.

The importance of culture is also reflected in the fact that 40 percent of all mergers and acquisitions fail, owing to problems in combining the workforces of the two companies. In such cases, individual leaders find themselves asking, "Am I playing in the system, on the system, or is the system playing me?" The system they refer to is not just company logistics, but one of cliques, clans, and coalitions. For example, the merger of AOL with Time Warner, which was initially welcomed as the sign of a new media concept, quickly stumbled, then faltered, owing to ongoing cultural clashes between the two companies over everything from which e-mail system to use in the workplace to the relative importance of financial goals versus editorial independence

(Stellan 2001). Severe infighting among senior executives and stockholders finally resulted in the resignation of Steve Case, the former CEO of AOL, and the collapse of the merger.

Clearly, the solution to the current rising failure rates lies with both companies and individual leaders. For now, let's focus on the individual cultural leader.

Individual Reasons for Failure

While everyone's experience is unique, and it is human nature to try to delude ourselves into believing that we are immune to the types of cultural transition issues that affect others, there is a pattern among leadership failures, to include:

failure to build partnerships with key stakeholders

- failure to learn the company, industry, or the job itself
- failure to gain commitments from direct reports
- failure to recognize and manage the impact of change on people

The first key to making a successful transition is to recognize you are not accepting one job, but two. In addition to whatever duties are outlined in the traditional job description, cultural leadership entails fitting in with the new company and its unique culture. It is also important to acknowledge, up front, the difficulty of building trust in new relationships. Also, you must be prepared to be told you are wrong, perhaps daily. To succeed, cultural leaders must approach every new challenge with an open mind-set that enables them to acknowledge their own fallibility and be open to new ideas and an array of cultural perspectives. The key is to maintain confidence, independence, and vision in the midst of complex assimilation.

A February 2007 *Business Week* article argues the the key to leadership is listening. the transition from the Chrysler Group to become the director of marketing communications at Wal-Mart, she was filled with enthusiasm. In her words, "I get overly

excited. I wanted to hit the ground running. Go, go, go."
However, she quickly found it difficult to fit in, and was fired
within ten short months. While Roehm acknowledges many
personal mistakes, including moving too quickly and not
adapting to her new workplace, she also paints a picture of
warring fiefdoms and a passive-aggressive culture that was
hostile to outsiders. Wal-Mart, she says, "would rather have had a
painkiller [than] take the vitamin of change." Nevertheless, she
concludes, the importance of culture cannot be underestimated.
There is wisdom to be gained from her failure. The pace of
change is as important as change itself.

So, the first key to successful cultural leadership is a mind-set
of openness and not only an ability, but also an enthusiasm for
shedding one's own preconceptions and timelines. Cultural
leaders must remain flexible in order to look ahead and respond
to changing political realities within their organizations, as well
as in the external environment. This mind-set enables cultural
leaders to develop strong networks, adapt to other languages and
belief systems, and ultimately become the activators for change
within their groups.

In today's business world, cultural leadership is about
establishing networks: core groups of people you can rely on for
advice, advocacy, new ideas, and mentoring. This is more than
simply developing the traditional professional partnerships of the
past; cultural leadership entails continuously developing and
building ongoing relationships among diverse groups of
professionals in an array of industries.

In the modern business environment, characterized by global
connections and shifting populations, leaders must bring the
strength of cultural diversity into the mix. They cannot succeed
by recruiting professional associates into their circle based upon
preconceived notions of what a leader looks like. The pathway to
progress will be laid by extending your network to include as
many individuals as possible from a broad range of origins,
including geographic, ethnic, and social class.

Language and Beliefs

In cultural leadership, the word language should be taken metaphorically as well as literally. Beyond linguistics, language entails symbols and communication patterns that reflect norms, values, and beliefs.

For example, the aboriginal language of Australia consists of land symbols, such as the lizard, snake, or wind. In order to become a leader among Aborigines, an understanding of land symbols is critical to relate to and influence members of the group effectively. Similarly, leaders of Citibank must immerse themselves in the language of private, commercial, consumer, and investment banking. No matter how sophisticated or primitive the group, each has a set of symbols that must be adhered to.

At its essence, all language reflects the customs, values, and beliefs that have been formed within a group over time. Beliefs move people to act. They are trusted by the culture and often form the basis for action. Leaders must understand the origins of the belief systems of those who follow them and be able to incorporate these ideas into their language and actions. For example, the leadership at the Ford Motor Company honestly believes "quality is job one." Marketing slogans such as this often reflect deeply held beliefs within the corporate culture.

Group Dynamics / Tribe

Language is critical. Language serves as the foundation of group dynamics; it is the glue that binds the proverbial tribe together. In his recent bestseller, *Tribes: We Need You to Lead Us* (2008), Seth Godin defines a tribe as "a group of people connected to each other, to a leader, and to an idea." Cultural leaders must create an authentic and engaging following. They must understand the culture they lead and form genuine connections with those around them. While individual professionals throughout an organization make the work happen every day, leaders focus on creating the right strategies to achieve the big-picture goals of the organization.

Leaders are charged with formulating plans to outperform the competition, largely by developing new products and services to better meet the needs of the market. At the same time, however, they must engender among the workforce a shared interest in the common corporate goal and purpose. To do this, cultural leaders must understand group dynamics. To lead, they must stimulate the passions of their teams through a combination of visioning and straight talk. In addition to understanding the way in which certain groups within the environment were formed, they must appreciate the significance of group power and how it is dispersed. Cultural leaders must be able to serve as mediators and facilitators in order to leverage conflict as a means of moving the group forward—and at times, get out of the way.

Against this background, cultural leadership also entails recognizing that each group is made up of individuals who also have their own languages or beliefs. Cultural leaders know how to speak to and motivate each member by appealing to his wants and needs. This is the key to creating a meaningful followership. Thus, leaders must be well attuned to variations among national cultures as well as to corporate culture and group dynamics.

Today's work environment is becoming increasingly multigenerational, as the members of Generation Y (those born between 1981 and 2001 begin to outnumber the workforce's previous generation ofGeneration X'rs). Cultural leaders must be aware of differences among the generations and the special traditions of the younger generation in order to purposefully engage new thoughts and future progress. This awareness must start at the top and be emulated by middle management.

Section 2:

The Tools

Chapter 6

Managers and Leaders

Why We Need Both

Author Thomas Friedman explains, "In a flattened world, people are able to work together on more stuff than ever before." Indeed, the twenty-first century has already witnessed burgeoning new forms of cross-border collaboration in the form of outsourcing, off-shoring, open sourcing, supply chaining, in sourcing, and informing. Wireless technology, voice-over Internet, file sharing, and other technology-based capabilities have acted like steroids to turbo-charge these forms of collaboration to form a virtual global village. This recent experience has given rise to a multitude of questions for cultural leadership. For example, what does a "flat world" mean in terms of corporate diversity? Does the concept of diversity even hold up in a truly flat world? What is the relevance of globalization for the individual, the group, and the organization?

No longer does every idea, solution, or problem need to pass through ten middle persons who simply edit an already perfect solution and then present it as their own. In a flat organizational world, this ambitious and, frankly, dishonest model has no place. The best explanation of how flattening your organization can make you more efficient didn't come from a business person or economics professor; it originated from General James E. Cartwright, USMC Commander. General Cartwright stated:

> The metric is what the person has to contribute, not the person's rank, age, or level of experience. If they have the answer, I want the answer. When I post a question on my blog, I expect the person with the answer to post back. I do not expect the person with the answer to run it through you, your OIC, the branch chief, the exec, the Division Chief and then get the garbled answer back before he or she posts it for me. The Napoleonic Code and Net-centric Collaboration cannot exist in the same space and time. It's YOUR job to make sure I get my answers and then if they get it wrong or they could have got it righter, then you guide them toward a better way ... but do not get in their way.

At an enterprise level, there are pressing questions about what constitutes a workforce. What is the best way to develop effective teams, and what skills and competencies are required to shift from traditional command-and-control systems to connect-and-collaboration modes of operation? Within the context of globalization, business enterprises will be required to adapt culturally in order to set common goals and influence people toward their achievement. Robert House notes in *Culture, Leadership, and Organizations: The GLOBE Study of 62 Societies*, "As economic borders come down, cultural barriers will most likely go up" (2004). Therefore, leadership certainly will be critical. That's what gives companies direction—what drives them onward and upward to success. Without adequate leadership, companies of the twenty-first century will find themselves all dressed up with no place to go.

This popular observation should not be taken to mean companies can afford to overlook the need for top-rate management. With all the talk about globalization, there is a tendency to focus exclusively on leadership. There seems to be a feeling that leadership captivates us with the why and what, while management bores us with who, when, where, and how. Especially in the current economic climate, cultural leaders are touted as the visionaries, the thinkers, and the exceptional big-picture people who will inspire us to embrace their vision for the future.

Against this background, you may be getting the impression that managers are simply the people who cannot lead. They lack the big-picture vision, because they are too mired in the details of corporate routines and too busy organizing to be orchestrating. Let's take a step back and be realistic. It is actually the managers who get companies where they want to go. What good is a roadmap toward the future without an operational car to get there? In this context, managers drive the car that carries their organizations forward. Who's in the car? Passengers include a plethora of different cultures, diverse thoughts, diverse backgrounds, cliques, clans, and coalitions.

But wait—let's go back to that term diversity. No other contemporary term has garnered such a bad reputation. Within the framework of cultural leadership, diversity doesn't simply mean checking a box that says you have one African American, one Caucasian, and one Asian in your company; that would be the height of simplemindedness. Diversity, within our context, refers more to a variety of thought, backgrounds, beliefs, and perspectives.

Did you know a group of fifty employees of the same gender, race, and education level can be extremely diverse? It is very true. An African American man from Harlem, New York, with an MA in education and an African American man from Los Angeles with the same credentials can be as different as night and day. Cultural leaders must never make the shortsighted assumption that ethnicity defines diversity. It is a part of diversity, but only a part. Diversity is actually about the individual: his attitudes, beliefs, and ability to work well with others.

The successful companies of the twenty-first century will focus more on multiculturalism, or true diversity, in order to tap into the variety of knowledge sets and perspectives within their workforces. While the traditional image of success in the United States is still a young, white, heterosexual, Christian male, a recent study by the Hudson Institute for the U.S. Department of Labor projects that 85 percent of new entrants into the workforce over the next decade will be women, minorities, and immigrants. In other words, the majority of the workforce does not or will not fit the traditional characterization. Thus, it will continue to be increasingly important for leaders to ensure high levels of mutual respect in the workplace to create an environment that values differences. Rather than allowing a prevailing culture to dominate, leaders will support individuals in the expression of who they are and what they bring to the workplace.

Back to managers and leaders: in short, companies need both. Managing and leading are different functions that satisfy different, specific needs. Many new MBA graduates view leadership as higher in status than management. They set leadership as the ultimate career goal, with management lagging behind as the booby prize. In fact, both functions are equally important and neither is better than the other. Managers can lead, and leaders can manage.

Most companies today realize it is best to develop managers who enjoy their work and are good at managing and leaders who want to lead, rather than pushing unsuitable people into either of these roles. In a diverse work environment, the objective is always to focus on individual strengths. If a person excels at management, let him manage, but if he is a great leader, let him focus on leading.

At the same time, however, companies recognize that it is important to strike a healthy balance between management and leadership in their organizations. Enterprises of all sizes must have efficient management to administer, control, and continually improve structures and processes alongside effective leadership that innovates, develops, and inspires trust both within the organization and among external stakeholders.

Maybe the biggest difference between managers and leaders is the way they relate to other people; this sets the tone for most other aspects of what they do. However, cross-cultural awareness is equally important for both groups. In today's global and diverse work environment, management entails more than coordinating functions across time zones. While the playing field is flatter than ever before, it is also ripe ground for miscommunication, misperception, and stereotyping.

Stereotypes are generalizations or assumptions that people make about the characteristics of members of a group. For example, some studies show that people who live in the United States are generally viewed by people of other cultures as friendly, generous, and tolerant, as well as arrogant, impatient, and domineering. Similarly, people from Asian countries, like India, are seen as shrewd and alert, but reserved and sometimes subservient. Clearly, not all Americans are friendly or domineering, and not all Indians are shrewd or reserved. Individual members of any cultural or ethnic group vary. Therefore, operating on the basis of such generalizations can lead to miscommunications and lose-lose situations. For example, based on the assumption that Asians are good at mathematics, but generally reserved and subservient, a manager may not make the effort to draw out the views of a Malaysian participant at meetings. He may also overlook the Malaysian for promotion on the assumption that she would prefer operational work. In such circumstances, the company loses the human capital to be gained, while the Malaysian team member misses the opportunity to make her full contribution by stepping into a more policy-oriented role.

Managers have to relate well to a much broader and more diverse workforce in order to control, protect, and coordinate functions and accomplish tasks on time and on budget. At the same time, leadership is about influencing people and building deep levels of trust in order to articulate what matters most, set the direction for the company, and create new products and services to keep pace in ever-changing markets.

Although managing and leading are very different, there is overlap. Particularly in modern organizations, with flatter and less hierarchical organizational structures, some individual leaders contribute to managing and some managers also provide leadership. While the mix between managing and leading will vary from one individual to another, the important thing is their main function—they're either a leader or manager first.

Managers create stability and deal with the day-to-day realities of the workload. Leaders have a strong vision for the future, know how to stir emotions, and set lofty goals that inspire people to pursue them. As Warren Bennis (1989) notes, "The manager does things right; the leader does the right thing." He explains, "I tend to think of the differences between leaders and managers as the differences between those who master the context and those who surrender to it. There are other significant differences, and they are crucial." Bennis elaborates by drawing the following twelve distinctions:

- Managers administer, leaders innovate
- Managers ask how and when, leaders ask what and why
- Managers focus on systems, leaders focus on people
- Managers do things right, leaders do the right things
- Managers maintain, leaders develop
- Managers rely on control, leaders inspire trust
- Managers have a short-term perspective, leaders have a longer-term perspective
- Managers accept the status quo, leaders challenge the status quo
- Managers have an eye on the bottom line, leaders have an eye on the horizon
- Managers imitate, leaders originate
- Managers emulate the classic good soldier, leaders are their own person

- Managers replicate, leaders show originality

As this dichotomy shows, if a company has too much management and not enough leadership, there is a risk it will stagnate. Because managers may be preoccupied maintaining systems and watching the bottom line, they can easily miss changes in the external environment, such as technological advances, consumer tastes, attitudes, and culture. At the same time, too much leadership and not enough management may result in a breakdown in the day-to-day administration and processes needed to produce. In the period ahead, it is increasingly more important for companies to find the right balance between these two functions. Moreover, managers and leaders need to complement each other, while making a shared effort to adapt to the new, flatter world. Such an effort must include:

- **Global Diversity:** Focusing on diversity (culture, race, and perspective) is critical to developing a global business model that responds to the realities of a flat world.
- **Cross-cultural Skills:** All members of organizations need to function at a high level across cultural paradigms. The new gold standard for performance is the borderless person.
- **Understanding Globalization:** Dialogue throughout organizations must promote understanding of the flattening world and what that means for the market. As Friedman notes, "the world is flat but nobody has told the kids."
- **Influencing the Pipeline:** Corporations will need to stay abreast of technological developments and collaborate through partnerships in real time.

In a May 2009 *Business Week* article entitled *"The Dynamics of Leadership—Team Behavior,"* author Jim Collins details very distinct corporate red flags. These red flags, Collins argues, provide insight into whether an organization is rising or falling. The important element is not teamwork, but proper teamwork.

- **Teams on the way down:** People shield those in power from unpleasant facts, fearful of penalties and criticism for shining light on the rough realities.
- **Teams on the way up:** People bring forth grim facts to be discussed—"Come here and look, man, this is ugly"; leaders never criticize those who bring forth harsh realities.
- **Teams on the way down:** People assert strong opinions without providing data, evidence, or a solid argument.
- **Teams on the way up:** People bring data, evidence, logic, and solid arguments to the discussion.
- **Teams on the way down:** The team leader has a very low questions-to-statements ratio, avoiding critical input and/or allowing sloppy reasoning and unsupported opinions.
- **Teams on the way up:** The team leader employs a Socratic style, using a high questions-to-statements ratio, challenging people, and pushing for penetrating insights.
- **Teams on the way down:** Team members acquiesce to a decision but don't unify to make the decision successful— or worse, undermine it after the fact.
- **Teams on the way up:** Team members unify behind a decision once made, and then work to make the decision succeed, even if they vigorously disagreed with it.
- **Teams on the way down:** Team members seek as much credit as possible for themselves, yet do not enjoy the confidence and admiration of their peers.
- **Teams on the way up:** Each team member credits other people for success, yet enjoys the confidence and admiration of his or her peers.
- **Teams on the way down:** Team members argue to look smart or to further their own interests rather than argue to find the best answers to support the overall cause.

- **Teams on the way up:** Team members engage in debate, not to improve their personal position but to find the best answers to support the overall cause.
- **Teams on the way down:** The team conducts "autopsies with blame," seeking culprits rather than wisdom.
- **Teams on the way up:** The team conducts "autopsies without blame," mining wisdom from painful experiences.
- **Teams on the way down:** Team members often fail to deliver exceptional results and blame other people or outside factors for setbacks, mistakes, and failures.
- **Teams on the way up:** Each team member delivers exceptional results, yet in the event of a setback each accepts full responsibility and learns from mistakes.

What is undeniable is that all teams on the way up operate in a flat world—a world that says the best idea wins no matter whose idea it is. It is brutally honest for the sake of production, not for the sake of blame. So how does a manager or leader change the trajectory of a team on the way down to one on the way up? This only happens with effort intentionally and must be based on the seven activators mentioned in chapter 1. Let's first discuss words.

Chapter 7

Words Mean Everything

The Key to Every Door

Words are the most powerful tool available to anyone. Now, I understand this is a pretty bold statement, but I challenge you to find anything more powerful than words. Very seldom do we think about words in such a granular way. Consider this: the most important things are communicated through words. Your birth certificate, your death certificate, your bank account, and your verdict are all events defined by words. Many people on death row right now would be free if the jury simply came back with different words: not guilty instead of guilty, life in prison instead of death, and so on. The wealthy make and lose millions each day based on what the market does, as represented by the words Dow Industrials, Standard & Poor, and so on. If you understand the power of words, you will never use them the same way again.

What is the difference between a good cook and a great cook? Give them the same ingredients, the same kitchen, and the same cooking time, and the two meals can taste entirely different. The skill of what to use and how to use it can make all the difference in the world. Too sweet, salty, or spicy, and no one eats it. Balance is everything. Words are no different.

But words have a very important partner: timing. It's not enough to simply understand what to say and how to say it—you must know *when* to say it. The cliché "timing is everything" should really be "timing affects everything." The time you choose to hire, fire, or critique is just as important as how you do these things. So how does this help you be a better cultural leader? The answer is simple.

Understanding how the elements of words and timing oscillate given different societies is a part of cultural leadership. No single approach is appropriate when speaking to every group. A leader must know the makeup of the groups and the people represented. None of the guidance delivered in this book will create great cultural leadership if delivered in the wrong container of words and timing.

People listen to what you say, and they listen to what you are trying to say. For this reason alone, today's leaders must know the words that touch the sensitive areas of culture. Words can inspire and do what nothing else can do. It is a mistake to diminish the content of speech as merely inspirational. As previously stated, inspiration is magical. When inspired, people are moved to do what they wanted but lacked the motivation to do. When inspiring a division manager to hit target sales numbers or meet production goals, leaders do not encourage shady dealings or lower work safety standards. Instead, they appeal to employees to give it all they have and rise to the challenge. The cultural leader must inspire with words.

Inspiration lives beyond the board meeting or the corporate rally. Inspiration keeps you up at night thinking about how things can change. Inspiration turns an idea into action and action into discovery. Ideally, cultural leaders seek to reveal to their audiences a uniquely inspiring vision. One vision accomplished can literally change the world.

Words Helped to Win the White House

"Yes, we can," at first glance, doesn't jump out as the most inspirational phrase ever spoken. But look a little closer. The most hated word in the English language is no. The most selfish word in the English language is I. And the most discouraging word in the English language is can't. Now, look again at the Barack Obama presidential campaign slogan. Do you see it now? Do you recognize the power this simple phrase holds? In three words, Obama related the will, unity, and ability to deliver the American dream. The three words, "Yes, we can," inspire positive emotions. By changing "I" to "we," millions of Americans united to accomplish what looked impossible. This is why words are so vital. Words breathe life. Think back on the individuals who truly changed your life. What were the elements of character that left a lasting impression on you? Perhaps they believed in you, supported you, and provided constructive criticism and positive feedback.

Imagine if, for one day, every company in the world communicated to their employees belief, ability, and support. What would sales look like for that one day? I believe they would go through the roof. Somewhere down the line, some stereotype—or worse, some knucklehead—convinced us that being in charge involves controlling, dictating, stepping on the spirit of others, and looking down our nose on those lower down the ladder by lacking confidence in their ideas and abilities. That mentality will not survive in our new world.

The positive results of inspiration, motivation, and support are incalculable. When you find out what pushes your constituency to achieve, the positive consequences can be enormous. Let's look at a few strategies you can use to better your words, your timing, and your effectiveness.

These strategies include:

- Define your purpose
- Communicate clearly
- Understand what motivates

Define your purpose: Your purpose, within the context of leadership, must be bigger than you. In other words, the purpose of a cultural leader is not to make money or have the biggest company in the world, but to create value. Cultural leaders want to create value in products, services, and, most important, people. However, you can only create value when you are clear on your core purpose and are able to share it with others. Ask yourself the following questions to prompt insight on your core purpose:

- If I had no need for money, what would I do for the rest of my life?
- What one event has created the best memory in my life?
- What one event has created the worst memory in my life?

You may be shocked at what the answers reveal. Let the revelation move you toward your essential purpose.

Let us consider a sample response to the questions posed. Let's say you have painted since childhood for the simple reward of single-handedly creating something from nothing and redefining an empty canvas into a portrait of self-expression. Maybe if you had no need for money, you would paint every day for the rest of your life. So our answer to question one: painting.

Secondly, what one event has created the best memory in your life? A potential answer for many may be the birth of a child. Regardless of the years that have passed, you may remember the first time you held your child as if it were yesterday. Recall the transformative affect when you felt like you, your environment, the world were new as well. You felt young again. All the pains and problems, at least for the moment, disappeared in the cloud of happiness you felt. Answer to second question: birth of a child.

What one event has created the worst memory in your life? The answer here could very well be the loss of a loved one. Maybe the loved one was the only person who believed in you as a child, the impetus that got you to go to college, or even the one who raised you during a difficult time in your life. The loss of this individual caused a gap in your life that money, success, and power all fail to fulfill. Answer to the third question: loss of a loved one.

What does all of this really say? Is this simply an act of basic human emotions with no real impact on how we conduct ourselves on a day-to-day basis? Actually, these are the events that shape our lives. Once your life is shaped, it is never reshaped. It can be adjusted, modified, or renovated, but the shape remains the same. Your leadership is subject to this shape. Leadership is not an island. It is not learned at a business school. Rather, it is learned in small ways and experiences you gain from family, friends, and even enemies. College experiences cultivate and refine this shape, but make no mistake about it, the shape was created a long time before that.

Let's look at the answer we came up with to question one again: you love to paint. So why don't you change your perspective on your divisions, departments, and regions from an organizational chart to a canvas? Let your passion for painting design your picture of success. Instead of solving lagging sales numbers, why not view sales gaps as areas that need to be filled in by, well, green? This may sound corny, but stay with me.

In our example, your best memory was the birth of your child. The reasons for this are based on newness, fresh starts, and hope for the future. Questions you should ask yourself: Do you leverage these on a daily basis? What are you creating? Are you simply managing?

Now, look at your business challenges. Instead of using what exists to solve what is in front of you, why don't you create something new to solve these problems? Creating something new will give you a refreshing feeling of hope and motivation and will even show those above you that you can solve tough problems with new ideas.

Business processes are notorious for moving around pieces of a losing game and calling the game new. Managers that fail in one department are given parallel positions in other departments, and, not surprisingly, failure resurfaces. Solution: go back to your first love and infuse this into your business model.

The worst time in your life was the loss of a loved one. Not just any loved one, but an individual who started you down a path of productivity, including the education that is the result of where you are today. Even the highest level of accomplishment cannot reduce this loss. Indeed, the more successful you are, the more you regret that this person will never witness the success they inspired. How can this help guide your day-to-day activities? Be that significant person for another. Give back. Nothing feels better than mentoring a young protégé in the same manner. This isn't sappy, cry-on-my-shoulder stuff. This is the initiative to amplify the good you recognize in those around you, constructively critique things that they must change, and have patience to allow them to change, just as someone did for you.

The concept of encouragement doesn't fit well within mahogany boardrooms, private jets, and spa treatments in Paris, but cultural leadership is different. The cultural leader pipes back the rhetoric of "I am somebody" and gives a little room for "You are somebody." The cultural leader brings everybody to the party, allowing for a sky full of stars versus a single shining star.

Communicate Clearly: Clear communication is the surest way to accomplish productivity. At times, clear communication is blunt; at times, it is cryptic. Clarity does not infer transparency; it infers effectiveness. For example, if you saw a man walking into the street without noticing an oncoming truck, you may scream, "Watch out!" If the man hears you and avoids getting hit, then your communications were abundantly clear. Clarity should only be judged by whether it works. Keeping it pretty isn't always the key; the point is to communicate effectively.

People are accustomed to listening to convoluted speech. Clear communicators can at first seem a bit harsh and possibly come off as too blunt. Cultural leaders understand this and must not bombard an audience with too much straightforwardness. Clarity is a process; allow the process to slowly unravel until nothing else but clarity is expected.

Understand what motivates: It is infinitely more productive for a person to work from their own motivation versus one given to them. That said, most people need a little nudging. We know there is no lack of motivational speakers. Many of them promote the useless and promise what can never be delivered. However, this does not undermine the true need for motivation. Motivation includes three main elements:

- Connect
- Acknowledge or respect
- Call to action

Connect: Discover what matters to your audience. Once again, answer the three questions addressed in "Defining your Purpose." If you had no need for money, what would you do for the rest of your life? What one event has created the best memory in your life? What one event has created the worst memory in your life?

Acknowledge or respect: Once you have connected, you can acknowledge the validity of a person's history, aspirations, and cultural makeup. There is another word for acknowledgement: respect. Respect goes a long way toward creating motivation. People don't want to do anything for someone who doesn't respect them. Granted, they may do the work because they have to, but the passion needed for extraordinary results will not be present.

It has always amazed me how many leaders subscribe to the theory of "beat down to build up." If you are training horses, this may work, but humans will find a way to undermine your leadership at the first available moment if you use such tactics.

Respect has a magical quality because it places an intangible responsibility on the receiver to live up to the honor given. Of course, this doesn't always work. For some, respect is the fuel used to further abuse others, but this is not the case for most. The cultural leader not only receives respect, but also gives it away in a greater portion. When respect is the foundation of a relationship, motivation is an easier sell because motives are not questioned. This takes time and doesn't occur the first day on the job, but you can start laying the foundation of respect on that first day.

Call to action: After the first two elements are accomplished, this phrase takes on a different sound. In fact, people want to follow those they respect. They want direction and will ask you for it, if at first it isn't given. The bottom line: take an organized, inclusive approach to your leadership, and you will be truly amazed at the increased results.

Once you have connected, acknowledged, and laid a foundation of mutual respect, the call to action is an easy sell. This cannot be contrived. Any action birthed out of impure, self-centered motives will be seen and perceived as such. This means you cannot follow a twelve-step plan to cultural leadership unless you engage first in an internal inventory of your true motives.

The Magic of Praise

The cultural leader never underestimates the power of praise. One of the most underused tools in leadership today is encouragement in the form of authentic feedback. Not fluff, not filler, but real, bona fide commendation of performance. Remember, cultural leadership is based on connecting, and part of this connection is praise. There are rewards that can be given, such as financial gain in the form of bonuses for performance, but public praise can be a low-cost strategy for elevating all aspects of an organization.

Sometimes leaders forget that people are just people. Behind all the degrees, experience, and hype lies a core need to be recognized, respected, and uplifted. Cultural leadership takes the time to praise associates in front of other associates, not in a way that creates envy, but in a way that creates cohesion.

It has always amazed me how many leaders understand processes, strategies, flow charts, and projections, yet overlook the most profitable element of any organization: people. People will make or break your organization. Whether your organization makes widgets or is in charge of heading a political campaign, people remain the manifestation of your plan.

Notwithstanding different management styles, praise and encouragement communicates effectively in every language. Start doing it! Not to make friends, but to make unison. We don't forget those who have inspired us. Life can get busy and cause us to procrastinate on showing appreciation to those who deserve it the most. Cultural leadership understands this. Cultural leaders use words of encouragement and display understanding to secure their connection with those with whom they must work and depend upon. This is not only good business, but also a good strategy. Never get so busy growing your business that you forget to grow your people.

Chapter 8

Do You Understand Who You Are Leading?

Pigskin Wisdom

Great football coaches have varying methods of establishing credibility. Generally, the more talented the player, the more difficult it is to establish credibility. Arrogance, entitlement, insecurity, self-esteem, and dominance can all exist on the same team, even in the same person, and create turmoil for every member of the group. This is interesting, because despite the distinct challenges, the group is still called a team with one mission: to win.

How do you coach someone who has more talent and ability than you ever had? How do you gain the respect of those who are bigger, stronger, and faster than yourself? How do you critique a group of physical specimens and convince them of the superiority of your advice? You must first understand who you are leading. Understanding cultivates authority and credibility. Understanding sows the seeds of influence deep into the listener. Whether an athlete played for Vince Lombardi or Tony Dungy, interview him and you would hear a common theme: "Understood, Coach."

Good and successful coaches understand how to communicate, how to inspire, how to run a team, and how to win, despite the team's differences. In relation, cultural leadership is the art of coaching differences.

The Language of Understanding

Effective leadership hinges on effective communication: your words, your inferences, your gestures, and your demeanor. All of these make up the composite of whether the receiver authenticates or ignores your ideas, visions, or proposals.

Effective communicators can't be defined as those who articulate, enunciate perfectly, or phrase sentences in their grammatically correct order. Effective communicators can, however—and within seconds—take a real-time analysis of their audience, pulling on everything they've ever read or heard from friends and enemies alike. They can then estimate potential disagreements that will occur from what they are about to say, and ultimately speak words that inspire, calm, and educate their audience.

In 2008, Free Press released an incredibly presumptuous book by Shelby Steele of the Hoover Institute. The book was entitled *A Bound Man: Why We Are Excited about Obama and Why He Can't Win*. This book should be admitted into the Smithsonian, not for its academic prowess or creative thought, but because it represents a social demarcation, a type of social bookmark. Steele strikes an intriguing tone. Whether one agrees or disagrees with his premise is irrelevant. What matters is the fact that society didn't listen. Why? Because this is a new world; the envelope of racism is being challenged. The election of Barack Obama has turned Steele's book on its head. The question now is, "Who is truly bound?" The most apparent mistake is that Steele blatantly underestimated the power of communication.

In the book, many notable African Americans are strategically placed in one of two categories called masks. The first subcategory is bargainers and the second is challengers. In the book, Steele says that bargainers are those who give people the benefit of the doubt. For example, he says that blacks (the bargainers) say to whites (the challengers), "I will not use America's horrible history of white racism against you, if you will promise not to use my race against me" (2008, 74–75). He explains further that this gives many whites a way out: a strategy to free them from being associated with the sins of the past. He tags Oprah Winfrey, Bill Cosby, Sidney Poitier, and Michael Jordan as prototype bargainers (2008).

Challengers, in the words of Steele, assume white Americans are all racist until they prove otherwise (2008). He points out that challengers basically exploit white America to get things, quotas, set-asides, and so on as almost a never-ending penance toward resolving the racism of the past. Bargainers are described as strategists who can never tell you what their true convictions are. They can never expose their true personal beliefs, as this would remove the ultimate bargaining chip (2008).

There is, however, a hybrid position missed by Steele. One cannot assume cultural leaders like President Obama ignore the integrity of their convictions simply because these positions are unspoken. Much like a movie editor connects scenes to best tell a story over the length of a film, cultural leaders position themselves against the backdrop of people, places, and events and allow these situations to speak on their behalf. It is more effective to build a homeless shelter than to get on radio touting how one should be built. Cultural leaders communicate positions, not always with words.

How can a man with an African Muslim name like Barack Hussein Obama take New Hampshire and Iowa? It is a result of this hybrid communication. Call it bargaining or challenging, the central disturbance of Steele's book is this: strategy is used for every successful venture in every society. Whether you are marketing snack cakes, running a ground war in Iraq, or running for political office in America, we all use strategy— or should, if we want to win.

Is it dishonest for a company to hold secret its true mission to buy out the competition? Is it unethical for a military commander to covertly work against the opposition while smiling for photo ops? These are hard questions that many don't want to ask, much less answer. But these questions require us to be consistent in our definition of honesty. It is the depth of selective accountability.

Specificity is a misnomer, a red herring. Politicians are strategists, like field generals. The *New York Times* interviewed President Obama's former law students and found that conservative students thought Obama was one of them, while liberal students thought he was one of them. How should we analyze this? In a world of globalization, cultural leadership is a strategic function, but one that must be honestly deployed. There are no tricks, but there is strategy.

President Obama ran a campaign that posed a profound request of all Americans. It was to truly consider the lunacy of racial and ethnic bias. Very few have considered this outside of heated discussions, marches, and race riots. In many ways, those situations are not only unproductive, but push further any substantive discussion that we as a people might have. Obama has encouraged serious discussion not by talking, but by positioning—positioning whites, blacks, and Asians side by side. Political rallies, grassroots, and door-to-door events all have profound effects on the issue. He was being a cultural leader.

Have you ever had distaste for a place, person, or thing, but when you really think about it, you really don't know why? Funny, isn't it? People see themselves differently when different people are around them. They are forced to confirm or challenge bias and prejudice, not because of the EEOC, but because the need to uncover our common humanity is not easily ignored.

There are no racists in foxholes. Ask a soldier that barely made it back from war. The reality is, when bullets are flying and friends are dying, no one thinks about interracial marriage or rednecks. When a soldier is bleeding from shrapnel and a man of a different race shows up to save him, all prejudice oddly evaporates, if only for a moment. But those are situations of panic and despair. This same concept should work in times of peace and calm.

Something weird happens when two families of different race see their respective children playing together. It challenges us in a good way, much like that foxhole. Our common humanity asks us, "Now why do I feel this way or that way about a certain group?"

The question nudges at you, and the job of a cultural leader is to amplify that nudge. The issue may be race, gender, education, or many other variables. Cultural leadership harnesses the best of this sentiment, includes everyone, and encourages us to embrace our common humanity.

Shelby Steele and the Delicacy of Crow

You may be wondering what Steele's response was to an overwhelming presidential win by Barack Obama. On November 25, 2008, Peter Robinson of the Hoover Institution interviewed Steele. Robinson posed this very question, asking Steele why he expected Obama to lose. His answer: "I thought he would have a difficult time winning because he never really revealed who he was." Aside from this being a pedestrian argument for a very devastating defeat of his book's premise, this answer is intellectually dishonest.

I am taking time to dismember this misguided view because its parts are very revealing. This old thinking paired with the old assumptions is dead. The vote for Barack Obama was as much a cultural vote as it was a democratic one. Only simplemindedness would bring the rotten trappings of prejudice and bias to a conversation about Obama's success,. Culture is more than race and ethnicity. Culture represents the *human* race.

Imagine walking into a beautiful, Biltmore-like mansion. Now, imagine a living room with an eighty-foot ceiling with gorgeous at first glance, multicolored draperies that extend from the floor to the ceiling. The bottom of the draperies has tassels that are identical. These tassels are worn and tattered, but nevertheless, identical. Everybody wants to climb the ladder and see what's at the top for a chance to catch a glimpse of how beautiful it is. Many think they can bypass the tassels, not realizing the tassels represent culture. The only place to connect is at the bottom, not the top. Connect at the bottom, with the homeless, the middle class, the underprivileged, and you can connect with everyone above.

The human race all touch at the bottom. This is where culture is born; this is where it thrives, where it is authentic. Touch the bottom and you touch everyone else.

Trust Builds Trust

The essence of leadership is trust. Service, humility, charisma, and vision are all necessary, but some leaders have only one or two of these characteristics and are still effective. No leader can survive without trust. Leaders must be trusted and must trust those working with them. Ironically, trust can be the last element to fully emerge. Leaders have been known to take charge through power, vision, and even education, but trust will not be manipulated. No leader can walk in the door and be trusted on day one. This must be earned not through actions, but inactions.

Yes, trust is earned by what is *not* done. Trust is counterintuitive. For example, trust is earned when an opportunity is presented that will secretly enrich the leader, yet he doesn't take the bait. Trust is earned when taking advantage of a young female executive would be accepted, yet the leader refuses. Trust illuminates a leader, making his influence greater with each passing day.

All things being equal, trust always breaks the tie. If you need surgery and there are fifty doctors with the same amount of education and same years of practice, whom do you choose? The one you trust. The one you've been going to for years. The one that knows your medical history and, most likely, some of your personal history. Trust is intangible, very difficult to define, but you know it when you see it. Any leader desiring to truly take the mantel of cultural leadership must be trustworthy.

President Obama benefited from the lack of trust in the former administration. In reality, Barack Obama hadn't been on the world stage long enough to have established a general feeling of trust among Americans. However, there was an odd dynamic at play. You see, trust can be established as an outcry of a previous violation of trust. For example, imagine you were running away from a knife-wielding killer chasing you through the streets of your local town. You turn the corner and you see a stranger cutting his lawn.

You immediately run up to the stranger yelling for help and requesting he take you into his house and call the police. Never once do you consider that the man cutting the grass could be just as dangerous as the man chasing you. You make an immediate risk/reward analysis that the stranger is most likely less dangerous to you than the man chasing you with the knife, and chances are, you are right.

Admittedly, this example is a bit exaggerated, but many people saw former President Bush as the man with the knife. And Obama? Well, he was just cutting the grass. Still, President Obama has to establish trust throughout the world, which will take time.

Trust is not a one-way street, and in order for leadership to truly work, leaders must be able to trust those working for and with them. This can be rather complicated, and cultural leadership can be greatly tested when met with competing interests. Leaders who listen give a voice to the voiceless, adapt and assimilate to multicultural surroundings, and may be powerless against political undercutting, tricks, and traders. This is where trusting your team becomes vital.

A team that supports the leader, his vision, and his philosophy may be the only protection a leader has against schemes designed to undercut his influence. Cultural leaders are not exempt from attacks, but the difference is, cultural leaders have more weapons at their disposal to fight attacks—in other words, more troops in the field.

Cultural leadership in this way can be the safest place a leader can occupy, like when we spoke of Osama bin Laden in the first part of this book. When you sow seeds of understanding and consideration among multiple races, ethnic groups, and gender, you expand your ground defenses. You extend your territory, making it more difficult to be surprised by an attack. Trust builds trust; it also builds protection.

Analyze, Implement, and Adapt

The experienced chess player asks himself three questions before making a move: Where am I now? Where do I want to go? How do I get there? Asking these questions, and getting the right answers, will not only better your chess game, but also your business game.

We are living in a unique time where historic institutions that were around for decades have now vanished from the corporate landscape as if they never existed. One has to wonder if these companies ever stopped, reviewed their processes, and asked those simple chess questions. It takes courage to ask the hard questions; it takes greater courage to adhere to the answers.

It takes greater courage because human nature is averse to learning of risks associated with encountering undesired events, no matter how damaging these events may potentially be. For example, millions of people travel by airplane each day, yet the portion of the flight where the flight attendants instruct us what to do in case of an emergency remains emotionally and intellectually unwelcomed. On one hand, this information is vital to surviving should an emergency occur; on the other, there is an unfounded feeling that learning how to survive an emergency somehow elevates its probability.

Organizations have traditions embedded into the very thought process of each and every operation. They can see the world around them changing, but somehow think it will never happen to them. In fact, many organizations, just like the passenger who sleeps through the emergency flight instructions, think nothing catastrophic will ever happen. This is why such companies are no longer in business.

Success is very deceiving, and long-term success can be deceit at its highest. Why would a company founded in 1920 have to change for this thing called globalization? Why would companies like IBM overhaul internal practices to fit more naturally in a diverse world? It is because no matter how successful a company is, the company is no competitor for the largest company of them all: the world. Either organizations will change willingly or the world will change them forcibly. Either way, change is going to happen.

Today, companies must not only face the inevitability of economic turmoil, but also social upheavals. The only prudent strategy is to face these changes head-on by establishing a preparatory, multicultural mind-set to be infused and normalized in day-to-day corporate operations. The world is changing at such a rapid pace that organizations cannot design customized strategies. They must instead generate a customizable framework to address the new face of a global world, economy, and workforce. Organizations must establish three key elements:

A framework for greater cross-cultural input

- A communication strategy that motivates and inspires *all* members of your organization
- A flexible strategy that assumes constant market change

Whether one believes globalization is an opportunity or a threat, it is a fact of life. The most effective way of dealing with this reality is with a pragmatic, disciplined approach. An approach of systems designed around a robust, resilient, and responsive cultural framework upon which all business operations can be based. In this way, companies reduce the chances of being unprepared for a dynamic workforce.

Prior to engaging in analysis for systematic change, organizations must acknowledge the cultural inefficiencies existent in their operation. Acknowledging outdated thinking is a prerequisite to a comprehensive reassessment and implementation of our suggested framework.

One of the best ways to combat this thought stagnation is to start planning offsite, strategic checkup meetings with the thought leaders in your organization. It is wise to include a third-party strategic cultural planning consultant in this meeting.

This time can be used not to simply talk, but for "what if" scenario creation, to creatively think ahead, and come away with substantive, actionable ideas of how to expand your relevance in the face of a new multicultural environment. This meeting can be used to establish the initial framework using cultural and quantitative tools that add credence to the takeaways.

It is said that success leaves clues; that means find them. Several companies have successfully managed crises and even profited during the worst market cycles. Studying how companies have succeeded during financial turmoil (depression, global market crashes) can be insightful as we attempt to build a stable cultural leadership environment. What is the relevance? Turmoil doesn't affect buildings; it affects the people in them. Houses aren't foreclosed; families are. In establishing cultural leadership, it is key to understand how cultures react to enormous stress.

One of the most difficult challenges for any leader is leading during a crisis. Happy days and sunshine takes care of itself. No one has to prepare for managing a department in which everyone is happy with performance compensation, responsibilities, work hours, and offices. The true character of a leader is only revealed under spontaneous volatility that necessitates difficult decisions be made in a hurry. In the words of an old southern grandma, "Birthday parties don't build character."

This is why it makes sense to take a moment to review the technical and qualitative aspects that over the years have allowed some companies to thrive during times of economic turmoil. We can learn from successful structures.

Dr. Roch Parayre, senior fellow in the Mack Center for Technological Innovation at the Wharton School, remarked, "Over eighty percent of all corporate failures in the west are not the result of a September eleventh type of crisis, they are the result of a slow burn, death by a thousand cuts where one cut doesn't kill you but the sum of the cuts makes you bleed to death ... you wake up and it's too late."

The world has become an increasing collaborative environment, an open architecture of intellect where corporate flexibility is highly regarded and rewarded. This flexibility is only second to the rate with at which it can be deployed into the marketplace. This rate can be the difference between enterprise growth and insolvency during times of turmoil. This moves us beyond the theory of how things should be, because even the best of theories are irrelevant when the storm hits. Weathering financial storms on a global scale requires practical, actionable processes that have been established in a pre-crisis atmosphere of calm. Learning them is not enough; we must act on what we have learned. This action requires us to challenge long-held corporate practices and test them against a new global model to uncover faulty reasoning that can result in faulty corporate practices.

Chapter 9

The Activators

Foresight – Ability to Connect – Relevant Communication

Tools for Cultural Change

As noted previously, in the current global marketplace, it is not uncommon for organizations to rely on multicultural teams working in a variety of locations. Even in traditionally homogeneous locations, workforces are becoming increasingly diverse. Therefore, companies across the world are placing increasing emphasis on cross-cultural awareness in an environment characterized by unrelenting pressures to raise production and reduce costs. Against this background, the GLOBE studies were conducted by the Wharton School to examine cultural dimensions that affect leadership in the workplace and "to determine the extent to which the practices and values of business leadership are universal (i.e., are similar globally) and the extent to which they are specific to just a few societies" (House et al. 2004). As a part of the studies, 170 researchers collected and analyzed data from interviews with seventeen thousand managers in sixty-two societal cultures around the world over a twenty-year period.

This study found that while the profile of an ideal leader may look different in different places, there are numerous shared leadership characteristics that apply across regions and cultures. These commonly held universal characteristics are seen as contributing to outstanding leadership in virtually all cultures and societies. They include the observation that an outstanding leader is expected to be encouraging, motivational, and dynamic, and that he should have foresight and be business savvy and maintain high levels of personal integrity.

Mediocrity is passive; productivity is intensive and purposeful. Cultural leaders' actions start a ripple of excellence with the intention of affecting an entire organization. Leaders must cultivate the correct social and psychological tools to systematically disassemble outdated approaches and implement solid practices. This all starts with foresight.

Foresight – Seeing the Future Now

In many ways, the difference between an architect and a builder is foresight. The architect stands on an empty, overgrown piece of land and sees a resort with thousands of people enjoying themselves. He then sits down and maps this vision into a language that can be translated into brick, steel, and metal. The skilled builder executes the vision. Builders materialize the design on the blueprint.

In his book *The Foresight Principle*, Australian futurist Richard Slaughter puts forth valuable thoughts as they relate to the importance of foresight. Futurists track relevant trends, analyze them, and think creatively about their direction and meaning. They do not *predict* the future; they *project* the future (1995). Slaughter defines foresight as the "deliberate process of expanding awareness and understanding through future scanning and the clarification of emerging situations" (1995, preface xvii).

Slaughter further describes foresight as "the discipline of assessing the possible consequences of actions and anticipating problems before they occur" (1995, preface xvii). A leader with foresight is admitting his inadequacies, which is healthy to do. Foresight is a form of expected optimism, and a good leader recognizes it as such. A leader with strategic vision can better foster collaboration, open channels of communication, and cultivate the organizational culture needed to guide the company through present challenges and future opportunities.

Foresight isn't "happy talk" about things and situations that have no place in reality. Leaders with authentic foresight are like farmers who can look beyond the current cold season and bad harvest to see the ripe potential just beneath the dirt. They know it will take time to separate the wheat from the chaff, but are fully confident that their people, their talent, and their organization carry the seeds of greatness in them. And so they water, and water, and water their vision, even in dry seasons, for what can and will eventually be. An effective cultural leader will not only understand and communicate with leadership and executives, but with the entry-level and housekeeping employees as well.

Often called "visionary" in the literature (House and Aditya 1997; Brodbeck et al. 2000), the universal leadership characteristic associated with foresight refers to a style of thinking that focuses on the future and provides a vision that inspires followers to take decisive action. This type of leadership goes beyond mere strategic planning. It uses foresight, teambuilding, and cultural understanding to launch initiatives that give companies competitive advantages. As Ireland and Hitt (1999) point out in their book, *Strategic Management: Competitiveness & Globalization*, this style of leadership rests on "a person's ability to anticipate, envision, maintain flexibility, think strategically, and work with others to initiate changes that will create a viable future for the organization" (43).

Rather than focusing on day-to-day operations, visionary leaders have made a fundamental shift in thinking that makes decisions based on a company's long-term goals. Rather than simply discussing current operational issues, these leaders bring to light assumptions about the future and how those assumptions shape the organization's decisions and strategies. These leaders stay abreast of developments in the global marketplace with a view for determining how their industries will be affected. This enables them not only to avoid mistakes, but also to grasp new opportunities as they arise.

For example, while IBM was focused on maintaining its position as the leading mainframe computer manufacturer during the 1970s, its leadership did not consider the potential market for personal computers. Meanwhile, Apple's executives were envisioning a computer for every man, woman, and child across the globe. This foresight enabled Apple to develop the laptop and take full advantage of the demand for greater flexibility and mobility in personal computing. As Gary Hamel and C. K. Prahalad (1996) note in their book *Competing for the Future*, "At worst, laggards follow the path of greatest familiarity. Challengers, on the other hand, follow the path of greatest opportunity, wherever it leads" (19).

Although the literature on strategic planning has always emphasized the importance of foresight, this universal characteristic is especially critical in the current global crisis. The current global economic downturn marks a period of significant change that will bring greater business opportunities on one hand and greater business challenges on the other. This is a critical moment for leaders to move beyond the focus on narrow interests and immediate problems, to reexamine the bigger picture. The crisis clearly points to a need to reexamine core assumptions about the marketplace and to take a fresh look at the skills, technologies, contacts, and products needed during the period to come. Most important, it will be critical to leverage that knowledge to rebuild it better, not only in terms of revealing and acknowledging current weaknesses, but also revitalizing organizations from the ground up.

The market leaders of the twenty-first century are currently reevaluating worldwide market opportunities. Based on a careful assessment of comparative advantage and country-specific conditions, including political and financial stability, these leaders will put plans in place, either to locate new markets for their company's goods and services or to increase economies of scale in existing markets.

Visionary leaders understand finance, marketing, human resource development, and international strategies. They not only comprehend, but tend to focus on issues that process-oriented leaders overlook; for example, the relationship between monetary value and exchange rate creating opportunities to increase market share, and how to keep prices and market share constant and reap additional profits (Aliber 1971).

Perhaps most important, visionary leaders look to the future with a view to moving their organizations ahead in ways that maximize opportunities. This is especially important in tough economic times, because having a positive outlook helps to generate confidence. Given the current tight financial conditions, investors and lenders will favor companies that project a positive spirit and a clear path forward. These companies naturally project, to customers, vendors, business partners, lenders, investors, and shareholders, a positive outlook and a strategic vision of future success.

Ability to Connect and Engage

The ability to connect and engage with others and to display genuine empathy is a cornerstone of global leadership. This characteristic is a catalyst for effective communication, teambuilding, and conflict management. It is the ability to identify with the needs of others and to engage diverse groups in the achievement of shared goals. In today's fast-paced business environment, the ability to genuinely connect with others is a prerequisite to success, especially as the rapid expansion of markets and organizations across national borders can leave organizations vulnerable to misunderstandings, cultural misinformation, and poor coordination.

Contrary to popular management theories, it is better to connect personally than professionally. Let me explain. Leaders are beginning to realize we are living in an age without precedent. Hubris has lost its shine. The humble yet confident genius has replaced the loud-talking executive dictator; nobody has use for that guy anymore. The successful military, corporate, religious, and tribal leaders alike have all learned one thing: connection breads loyalty. Think about this. Everything that works in your home, car, office, and even your body works because it is connected. You connect by listening to what is said and what is not, by never being too busy to look into the eyes of the person with whom you are speaking, and lastly, by affirming admirable characteristics and instructing people out of bad habits instead of criticizing them for them.

One thing is for sure—the Asian accountant, the Caucasian engineer, and the African American IT director pay the same for groceries at the local store. This example shows more connection than disconnection, regardless of race or occupation. In many ways, the ability to connect is fulfilled when leaders understand how much is already connected. And so leaders must walk the line between the obvious and the unknown to find the answer. The great part about this is that the unknown becomes more obvious the more one connects, which feeds directly into relevant communication.

In the work environment, it is imperative for leaders to be able to think, feel, and communicate from the perspective of other shareholders, including workers, stockholders, suppliers, producers, and customers. As the saying goes, this is the capacity to virtually "walk in their shoes" and view the organization or the market from a variety of angles.

To empathize with another, one must first understand the other person's perspective and communicate that understanding back to him effectively. Thus, active listening becomes critical. Cultural knowledge and language skills are often needed to maximize the transfer of knowledge, which includes not only explicit information (verbal or written dialogue), but also implicit understandings (body language and tone of voice). Perhaps even more important is the establishment of a genuine emotional connection that serves as the foundation of trust.

The development of empathy involves a three-step process. It begins with a sincere concern for others, including a genuine interest in their situations and perspectives. The second step is active listening aimed at learning. The third step entails an in-depth understanding of different viewpoints. This does not necessarily mean agreeing or embracing every opinion, but it does mean genuinely considering and respecting opposing positions. The process of connecting and engaging, or establishing empathy, can be particularly challenging in multicultural environments where language differences can confound communications. In such environments, there is a need to be mindful that any misunderstanding can give offense. Therefore, an inability to engage and connect can create a huge barrier to effective leadership (Gregersen et al. 1998). Fundamentally, an emotional connection is important because it leads to goodwill.

Employees who hold their leaders in high regard are more ready to give them the benefit of the doubt and put forth their best efforts, even in circumstances where this may entail personal sacrifices. In global organizations, where webs of interrelated units must cooperate and coordinate to meet customer needs, goodwill, rather than clear lines of command and control, is the force behind the achievement of business-related initiatives.

For example, the vice chairman of Huntsman Corporation, the largest privately held chemical manufacturing company in the United States, visits with each employee at least once a year. In the book *International Management Behavior: Text, Readings, & Cases*, Vice Chairman Hal B. Gregersen and Associate Professor of International Strategy and Leadership at Brigham Young University Jon Huntsman Jr. explain that the success of his company was built on leadership failures that had occurred at other companies (2000). Those companies included Eastman

Chemical, Hoechst Celanese, Monsanto, Shell, and Texaco. According to Huntsman, these companies' weaknesses were rooted in their leaders' failure to connect with employees and inspire commitment. Therefore, Huntsman and a team of senior executives at Huntsman Corporation visit each of the company's facilities around the world each December to personally meet with every employee. Huntsman says:

> In December, we are gone every single day before Christmas. We visit every Huntsman factory, every facility around the world. We shake everyone's hand. We talk to every spouse and child and learn about what they are doing. Where are you going to school? What do you like doing? Is your family happy? What can we do for you? We also give them each a holiday gift. Maybe it's a television, or a stereo, or a cruise. We want them to know how much we appreciate them. We want to make our employees feel they are the most important people in the universe. We honestly believe this. (2000, 107).

This initiative stems from Hunstman's genuine desire to learn about other cultures and personal circumstances, as well as a need to clearly understand employees' capabilities, motivations, and values. According to Huntsman, this knowledge, as well as the personal connections among employees, brings huge rewards to the company and creates goodwill. Moreover, it enables business-related insights and ideas to percolate up from the factory floor. Huntsman notes:

> Making these visits lets us connect with our people personally. We believe that the best ideas come from the factory floor. When people have met me, shaken my hand, and talked to me, they feel they know me. I challenge them by saying, "Here is my number. If you have a good idea, a

way to work more efficiently, call me." And they do! (2000, 107)

Relevant Communication

Of course, the ability to communicate effectively is critical in all business operations, but it is also the defining criteria for leadership. In their book, *Shared Leadership: Reframing the How and Whys of Leadership*, Craig Pearce and Jay Conger note:

> The ability to manage is measured by what you know, and what you get done, but your ability to lead is measured not only by your competence but also by your ability to communicate who you are and what you stand for. In this respect, global leaders communications reflect operational goals and methodologies, but also credibility, trustworthiness, confidence, passion, facts, and faith. (2003)

As we discussed earlier, communication represents the wheels that transport productivity. Without it, you'll get nowhere. For leaders to be relevant they must communicate in a way that matters. In order to communicate in a more meaningful, relevant way, there are a few things to remember. Communication must be:

- **Meaningful**

Meaningful communication is niche communication. It specifically applies to the person or people to whom you are speaking. Template-like phrases should not be used. Instead of speaking about a situation in generalities, relevant communication addresses elements that are pertinent to the person, business department, or activity.

- **Timely**

Ironically, timing can't necessarily be timed. It is usually the outgrowth from a pattern of awareness and an outgrowth of knowing your people—

their concerns, their likes, and their dislikes. It is only after such a relationship has been established that a leader can insert a word that seemingly was right on time, when in actuality, timing is the result of relationship.

- **Clarity**

To be a relevant leader, you must be clear about your motives or intentions. Intent is the one thing most difficult to fake. A person who has just lost his job can immediately pick up whether your words of consolation have been slightly dipped in glee or if you have true empathy for him. Clear words are underestimated, and many leaders take the path of hiding their intentions behind words and political phrases that lead the listener on a scavenger hunt to find out what is really meant.

Cultural leaders are honest, even about the fact they do not understand a particular culture. When a manager sincerely asks an employee to explain his culture, there is a bit of magic that occurs. Such an event plants the seeds for the relationship to grow and grow over time.

In the book *Powerful Conversations: How High-Impact Leaders Communicate* (1999), Phil Harkins defines communication as "an interaction between two or more people that progresses from shared feelings, beliefs, and ideas to an exchange of wants and needs to clear action steps and mutual commitments. Specifically, a powerful conversation produces three outputs: an advanced agenda, shared learning, and a strengthened relationship" (xii). As this definition suggests, communication should be seen as a four-step process that involves listening, questioning, thinking, and acting. First, explicit information is provided (listening); second, information is placed into context (questioning); third, information is internalized and reflected upon (thinking); and fourth, the information is acted upon (acting). Although this process can be learned and mastered over time, there are certain natural traits that bolster people's ability to become effective leaders and communicators.

Carte and Fox's book *Bridging the Culture Gap* says that these natural attributes include the ability to keep an open mind; the ability to genuinely empathize by putting oneself in the other person's position; and the ability to ask carefully chosen questions, both to gather additional information and to check that the assumptions and deductions made are correct (2004).

Thus, effective leadership communication begins first with what Pearce and Conger call invested listening (2003). This includes reading body language, intonation, cultural signals, professional signals, and corporate language. It requires not only patience, but also that the listener set aside any preconceived notions and opinions in order to hear the other person's perspective. It also entails checking in with the speaker occasionally to ensure he knows you are being responsive and acknowledging his feelings. It is also important to distinguish between your point of view and that of the speaker in order to highlight areas of common interest.

In this latter respect, effective questioning is used to make sure that the messages you have received are indeed those intended by the speaker. Thus, it is often helpful to ask nonthreatening, open-ended questions—namely those beginning with what, when, and why—to ensure you completely understand the driving forces behind the speaker's point of view.

In the book *How to Argue and Win Every Time*, world-renowned attorney Gerry Spence says that sometimes when he is listening to the final argument of his opponent, he lays his head back and listens only to the sounds. He explains that sounds always carry the argument better that the words. Sounds reflect the urgency, the sense of caring, the essence of truth, and the power that can change a jury's mind (1995).

Cross-cultural understanding really comes into play during the thinking phase of effective leadership communication. Simply put, communication styles tend to differ among different cultures.

Some cultures are more gregarious and some are more subtle. Some cultures prefer arguments based on cold logic. Others value intentions, while some engage in more formality.

As a leader, it is critical to develop a personal communications style that meshes with and balances the needs and expectations of each participating group. This is especially important in today's global environment where leaders are often working with virtual teams representing a diverse array of cultural backgrounds.

Personal leadership styles not only play to the cultural understandings of diverse workforces, but also serve to create and maintain corporate or organizational cultures. In organizational environments, the leader's communication becomes the visible expression of the cultural understandings inherent in the organization. This culture is often created, recognized, and passed on through stories, myths, rites, reward systems, and symbols.

When Winton Blount was named postmaster general under President Nixon during the reform of the Post Office Department in 1970, he was charged with transforming the organization from a government agency to a quasi-governmental corporation owned by the federal government.

He began the reform by using degradation to discredit the traditional motto "service at all costs" and removed more than two thousand older employees who had been agency's its champions. Then, because the image of the post office had been tarnished during lengthy legislative debates on the proposed reform, Blount changed the symbols associated with it.

Specifically, he changed the name of the organization, designed a new logo, and repainted mailboxes and trucks from drab olive to patriotic red, white, and blue. By changing these traditional symbols, Blount was able to communicate to both employees and a critical public that the U.S. Postal Service was a different organization than it had been in the past.

Closely related to the use of cultural forms and symbols are the traditions that their use originates and fosters. Cultural continuity requires that members of a group remember and pass on to new generations the ideologies to which they subscribe.

A prime example of the way in which ideologies are passed on through written and oral tradition is provided by Alcoholics Anonymous. This group publishes its own book, the *Big Book*, which recounts the stories of founding members, a widely known and revered set of guiding principles called the Twelve Steps, and many other documents setting forth the vision of the founder. Furthermore, as Trice and Beyer (1986) point out, "The activities of AA center around talk—and this talk frequently makes reference to the Founder and his testament" (149–150).

Storytelling plays an important role in any organization. It serves as a way to remove fear and establish clarity of purpose as new members join the group. Stories of past leaders and successes, as well as challenges, help to create a shared context. Passing on stories about an organization's history builds a foundation for decision making on a day-to-day basis, as well as one for innovation and change.

In the book *Squirrel Inc.: A Fable of Leadership Through Storytelling* (2004), Stephen Denning describes how storytelling is used to communicate vision, values, and knowledge to encourage group cohesion. He suggests there are nine steps involved in what he calls a "springboard story" (47):

1. The leader defines the specific change idea to be implemented in the organization
2. The leader identifies an incident (either inside or outside the organization, community, or group) where the change idea was in whole or in part successfully implemented
3. The incident is narrated from the perspective of a single protagonist who is typical of the target audience
4. The story specifies when and where the incident happened
5. In telling the story, the leader ensures that the story fully embodies the change idea, extrapolating the idea from the story if necessary

6. The story makes clear what would have happened without the change idea
7. The story is stripped of any unnecessary detail
8. The story has an authentically happy ending
9. At the conclusion of the story, the leader links the story to the change idea with phrases such as "What if ..." or "Just imagine ..."

Finally, whether through storytelling or other means, effective leadership communications are characterized by qualities of significance, values, consistency, and cadence (Baldoni 2003). These messages are significant in that they focus on big issues that reflect the present and the future direction of the organization, regardless of whether the subject matter focus is on people, performance, products, or services.

These messages are always designed to reflect and reinforce the organization's vision, mission, and culture. They are consistent in serving as an example of stated values and desired behaviors. Finally, they are conveyed with regularity and frequency throughout the organizational structure.

It is also important for all leadership communications, especially in cross-cultural contexts, to speak from the heart, avoiding sophisticated industry-specific jargon or complex vocabulary. Indeed, leaders that do well remember that people have widely different levels of ability. It is easy to assume that people have a deeper level of understanding of a language than they actually do. Therefore, it is best in cross-cultural contexts to stick with basic, simple words that everyone in the organization can understand.

It is also important to devise a communications program in ways that help everyone get to know everyone else. Clear policies for communication frequency and distribution are needed to ensure that knowledge is shared effectively. Virtual teams rely heavily upon frequent contact and need a way to develop a level of personal understanding even in the absence of physical interaction.

Chapter 10

The Activators II

Trustworthy – Dynamic Presence – Positive Attitude – Confidence Builder

Tools for Cultural Change Trustworthy

Throughout the scholarship on global leadership, there is nearly unanimous agreement that trust is an essential component of effective leadership across all cultures. As Barbara Misztal notes in her book *Trust in Modern Societies*, trust has three functions. First, it creates predictability and confidence in the normative aspects of the social order. In other words, the structure of an organization itself can be seen as a product of widely accepted norms prescribing trustworthy behavior (1996). Second, trust helps to reduce complexity. This is especially important in today's globalized society, where the consequences of individual decisions can have major effects across the entire organization and their respective departments (1996). Finally, trust is the lubricant for cooperation (1996). As Gregersen et al. (1998) show, people simply work harder and more cooperatively for leaders they trust. Moreover, a study by Sirkka Jarvenpaa and

Dorothy Leidner titled Communication and Trust in Global Virtual Teams found that high levels of trust actually reduce the significance of cultural differences (1998).

Webster's *Ninth New Collegiate Dictionary* defines trust as "assured reliance on the character, ability, strength, or truth of someone or something." Expanding on this concept, Mayer, Davis et al. (1995) note that trust can be seen as "the willingness of a party to be vulnerable to the action of another party based on the expectation that the other will perform a particular action important to the trustor, irrespective of the ability to monitor that other party." Put simply, trust is a lack of fear. However, in the business environment, fear can take a variety of forms: dismissal, punishment, loss of income, loss of prestige, or loss of power, among others.

Against this background, Lewicki and Bunker (1995) suggest that professional relationships are based on three types of trust: calculus-based trust, knowledge-based trust, and identification-based trust. Calculus-based trust is confidence in the system of potential rewards and punishments for adhering to or violating organizational norms. Identification-based trust is the extent to which leaders and followers are confident that there exists a mutual understanding of each other's wants and needs. Finally, knowledge-based trust is recognition of leaders' technical expertise and their ability to establish and accomplish organizational goals.

While trustworthiness is a universal leadership characteristic, there is a need to understand how trust is perceived in each particular culture represented in a work unit or an organization as a whole. Again, the aim is to balance perceptions in ways that give the broadest spectrum of stakeholders—including employees, board members, customers, suppliers, and investors—the highest level of confidence in the predictability of the organization and in the products and services it provides.

Although the professional reputations of leaders in terms of their technical expertise and experience are usually well-known, they still need to earn the trust of the groups and individuals they serve each and every day. In this respect, it is critical for leaders to adopt communication systems that reinforce their trustworthiness through the establishment of common business understandings and strong business ethics. In the book *Trust in Relationships: A Model of Trust Development and Decline* (1995), Lewicki and Bunker contend that breakdowns in trust lay at the heart of most conflicts; thus, the re-establishment of trust must be included as a key ingredient in any effort to resolve or manage conflict. They set forth the following as important steps in establishing and building trust:

- Agree explicitly on expectations of tasks and deadlines
- Agree upon procedures to monitor the other person's performance
- Cultivate alternative ways for needs to be met
- Increase awareness of how performance is seen, measured, and interpreted
- Share common interests
- Share common goals and objectives
- Share similar reactions to common problems
- Share values and integrity

Of course, the effort to build trust takes time, patience, and consistency. Unfortunately, destroying trust can take only an instant. As Gregersen et al. (1998) note, most executives describe integrity as ethical behavior and loyalty to their organization's agreed values and strategies. Their study found that both personal and company standards are more prone to be compromised overseas. This is because managers who are removed from corporate oversight are tempted to change their behaviors and their organizations' approaches to appeal to local values or demands. Despite the short-term advantages, the study shows that global leaders are most effective when they consistently maintain the highest ethical standards in personal and professional matters. When crossing cultural, national, or functional lines, consistency and personal integrity are critical in establishing and maintaining trust throughout an organization. The authors also emphasize that this often makes the difference between winners and losers in global competition.

Dynamic Presence

In addressing charismatic or dynamic leadership, Boal and Bryson (1988) indicate that the essence of transformational leadership is to lift ordinary people to extraordinary heights. Similarly, Bass (1985) says that transformational leadership is the ability to get people to perform beyond expectations. In other words, a dynamic presence reflects the ability to inspire the desire to follow, to inspire achievement beyond expectations, and to inspire people to risk change.

The term "dynamic presence" in leadership is used to describe someone with a unique essence and a positive way of presenting himself. It can be seen as a sense of optimism combined with a positive attitude. Some of the world's greatest leaders have been those who have withstood all types of challenges and adversities. Yet all great leaders share a positive attitude as a common trait. Dynamic leaders also know that they alone cannot make change happen. To lead any organization, leaders must have a "why not" attitude. They must be open to new ideas, resistant to negative attitudes or trends, and most important, not be afraid of change. Dynamic leaders throughout history have shared an ability to know what they wanted to achieve and the drive to go for it.

For organizations to thrive, leaders need to engage in a "can do" approach. The energy and optimism to seek out new ideas and opportunities and the fearlessness to take advantage of emerging developments and make them work in their businesses' favor is critical.

A major point in dynamic leadership is the inspirational process that leads to rewards. It can be generally assumed that most people will work for the organizational or corporate good. In some cultures, the group is more important than the individual. Rewarding people for a job well done is meaningful and important within any organization. People are motivated to do their best when they value the reward. So, it is important to know the receiver of the reward and to find out what rewards individuals and groups within a work unit or organization value most.

When it comes to rewards, sometimes recognition and appreciation are enough. Truly dynamic leaders make sure they know the individuals with whom they are working, and they evaluate the performance and the satisfaction of each individual on a case-by-case basis. At the same time, they ensure that the system is predictable and fair.

While effective leadership can be taught, charisma seems to come naturally for many dynamic leaders. These natural leaders genuinely enjoy what they do, and their organizations thrive because of it. In this respect, dynamic leadership should be defined in terms of the effect one has upon group behavior. Dynamic leadership has a great impact on shaping attitudes and behaviors. It can be measured by the performance of the group. This is because dynamic leaders relate with others in ways that seem to positively affect their organizations as a whole. A dynamic leader is an integral member of the organization whose goals he shares, and he has the ability to show others how to realize those goals. A dynamic leader encourages the people around him to do what they can do best and inspires them to want to do their best.

As the GLOBE studies show, leadership traits are distributed between authoritarian and dynamic leadership styles. An authoritarian leader holds power and domination as fundamental patterns of influence. The authoritarian manager uses his position, title, and authority as the primary means for motivating people to action. The authoritarian leader is not a dynamic leader and shows little confidence in others. The organization is controlled by tactics of intimidation.

In dynamic leadership styles, the leader is not interested in power, but in inspiring people to participate in the activities of the group. A dynamic leader has a strong sense of self and respects that sense in others. He has confidence in the organization's members. A dynamic leader encourages interpersonal relationships and puts the interests of the group above personal considerations. He plays a productive role in the positive behavior of others and leads organizational members in their individual pursuit of personal and organizational goals. Because a dynamic leader will appeal to the needs and best interests of the organization, he will tend to have a much more positive way of influencing the organization's functioning than would be the case under authoritarian leadership.

Based on these considerations, a leader will not be perceived as dynamic unless he considers the organization's individual and collective needs. Earning trust and respect is essential for any leader who desires to set a positive example. Dynamic leadership requires an individual to practice sound human relations at all times.

The organization's members will trust and respect a leader who shows an interest in them, both individually and collectively. People naturally want to follow leaders who are honest and who treat them with consideration. Too many leaders have tried to take an authoritarian approach in demanding respect from individuals and organizations. They will often resort to command-and-control approaches to increase production levels. Dynamic leaders know how to manage others more effectively because they have a better understanding of human behavior.

While some truly dynamic leaders are born, not made, most aspects of effective leadership are learned. Every high-performance leader should analyze his leadership style and continually develop the capacity to lead. To discover a more dynamic leader in yourself, apply the following inventory:

- Do you bring out the positive in your people?
- Do you have a "why not" outlook? Are you open to new ideas and different ways of doing things?

- Once a week, examine organizational process within your area of responsibility. Is there a more efficient or more effective way to do things?
- Do you have a positive attitude? Do others consider your attitude positive?
- When things get tough, do you see the glass as half empty or half full?
- Do you recognize and reward others for innovation and decision making?
- How do you show others in the organization that they are an important part of the organization?

Positive Attitude

One of the most important keys to productivity and effective leadership is having and maintaining a positive attitude. A positive attitude consists of having a clear vision for the future, taking pride in oneself and in the company, and engendering respect and trust. Nothing else has a greater effect on productivity and leadership ability than a leader's attitude.

Having a negative attitude or even a neutral one can undermine your own productivity and lead to mediocrity throughout the work environment. A positive attitude will help alleviate the frustration during periods when you are putting in lots of effort and getting little or no results.

When a leader has a less than positive attitude, it becomes difficult or impossible to put in place the kinds of systems that others want to follow. A positive attitude helps a leader look for solutions. It naturally leads to greater creativity, which in turn inspires work units and gets the best out of every member of the organization.

When a leader is negative, he will tend to see only the obstacles and become stressed out. Because of this example, other stakeholders in the organization will also become frustrated. In fact, when a leader is feeling a lot of stress, he cannot be creative or engender that "can-do" attitude that leads to innovation. Conversely, a positive attitude among an organization's leadership allows the business to thrive even in the face of seemly insurmountable challenges. This is because a positive outlook in itself inspires creativity and resourcefulness.

A leader with a positive attitude actually helps to alleviate stress throughout the organization because the leader's attitude determines how stakeholders perceive the organization as a whole. Thus, it either pulls the business up or down. Behaviors that create an atmosphere of competence and success, promote high expectations and confidence in followers, can inspire and motivate all the stakeholders in an organization.

Mary Kay Ash, the founder of Mary Kay Cosmetics, is a good example of the way in which a positive attitude and role modeling leads to effective leadership. Everyone who joins the Mary Kay company is given literature detailing the saga of how Ash's personal determination and optimism enabled her to support herself and her children as a saleswoman after her husband left her. Her personal positive outlook is clearly reflected in the company's slogan: "Women can succeed beyond their wildest dreams—if just given the opportunity." During elaborate meetings called Mary Kay seminars, employees receive her personal encouragement. They are inspired to identify with her and her ideology and are motivated to achieve high levels of sales and to earn public praise and valuable awards. All of these behaviors serve to motivate and guide employees throughout the organization to follow Ash's personal vision of optimism.

How does a leader turn a negative attitude into a positive one? The same way someone with a positive attitude maintains it. The leader needs to eliminate or reduce to a minimum all negative inputs, influences, and factors in the organization and introduce positive ones. If the leader has a positive attitude, the organization's outlook and its reputation will also become positive. The ability to maintain a positive attitude even in the face of disappointment is one thing successful business owners have in common. From Sam Walton to Bill Gates, effective leaders have kept positive attitudes even when overcoming huge challenges, and that factor alone has helped their organizations to triumph in the face of adversity.

Everyone knows that a positive attitude is beneficial. So, how do dynamic leaders use this knowledge? Properly utilizing the knowledge will determine the leader's level of success. One technique almost all good leaders use is care in choosing their associates and circles of friends. They know that if they surround themselves with negative people, their own outlooks will be affected, and that could infect the organization and inhibit growth and productivity. These leaders truly believe the phrase "attitude is everything" and that it applies to negative attitudes as well as positive ones. Leaders surround themselves with others who exhibit positive attitudes, because positivity in itself is contagious.

Even in today's harsh market, a positive attitude can work its way through any organization. Exhibiting a positive attitude helps dynamic personalities get the attention of those who are in positions of power. This is because effective leaders instinctively recognize, understand, and are drawn to people with positive outlooks. They also tend to reward those who exhibit positive attitudes appropriately. A "can do" attitude is necessary to be recognized as a valued employee in almost any business context. Taking the phrase "attitude is everything" to heart is absolutely essential if you plan to grow in your industry. It doesn't matter if your particular organization is a sole proprietorship, a small- to medium-sized enterprise, or a company employing thousands of people across the globe; the positive attitude expressed by leaders is reflected in their businesses.

If dynamic leaders consistently exhibit a positive attitude to their company stakeholders, the company will go the extra mile and the business will grow, no matter how competitive the environment. All dynamic leaders who have achieved success have given the same advice: acknowledge the presence of others in your organization, acknowledge and reward those with positive attitudes in the organization daily, and never fail to recognize positive attitudes in others.

Confidence-Builder

"Setting an example is not the main means of influencing another; it is the only means."

—Albert Einstein.

The ability to build confidence is an important aspect of transformational leadership. In the book *Organizational Dynamics* (1990), Bernard Bass notes that transformational leadership "occurs when leaders broaden and elevate the interests of their employees, when they generate awareness and acceptance of the purposes and mission of the group, and when they stir employees to look beyond their own self-interest for the good of the group" (21).

Leaders must earn the confidence of their employees in order to achieve these goals and accomplish effective transformational leadership. Some managers erroneously overcompensate when exerting power or authority, laboring under the mistaken belief that they must appear superior to earn confidence. Others stray too far in the other direction.

In a *Wall Street Journal* article, "In the Lead: How Cynthia Danaher Learned to Stop Sharing and Start Leading" (16 March 1999), Danaher revealed that she had been too forthcoming with her 5,300 employees in a speech as the new general manager of Hewlett-Packard's medical products group. She said in her speech, "I want to do this job, but it's scary, and I need your help." Three years later, Danaher admitted, "People say they want a leader to be vulnerable just like them, but deep down, they want to believe you have the skill to move and fix things they can't." She said that making employees feel comfortable must take the backseat to setting a clear direction as a leader .

James M. Kouzes and Barry Z. Posner identify five key leadership traits in their book *The Leadership Challenge* (2003):

1. Honesty
2. Forward-looking
3. Competent
4. Inspiring
5. Intelligent

These traits wield great influence in inspiring the confidence of others. It is not enough to simply have these characteristics; they are effective only when demonstrated consistently in noticeable ways.

Scandals are rampant in business, and with media pumping out the details online and in traditional media fourteen hours a day, people have learned to distrust authority figures. Therefore, today's leaders have to go out of their way to prove they are honest. Honesty can be accomplished by recognizing and correcting mistakes. Unfortunately, these situations are often mishandled. Too many would-be great leaders fear that owning up to errors or poor decisions will negatively influence others' perceptions of their ability. On the contrary, people generally respect a leader who has the self-confidence to admit his part in a mistake and take the measures needed to recover quickly and implement an effective solution.

The key is demonstrating. Most effective managers have an idea of where they are going and what it should look like when they get there. This is called forward-looking. However, many fail to share this vision with others. Effectively communicating goals, missions, and visions allows others to share in the excitement and inspires them to perform better as they understand why they do what they do on a daily basis. Communicating a forward-looking perspective does not mean explaining each aspect of the plan in detail or making promises or guarantees about the future. An overview of the leader's vision instills confidence and demonstrates his ability to manage the present while thinking toward the future.

Leaders by nature must be highly competent in any number of fields. The ability not only to accomplish each task, but also to lead others by demonstrating competence in a variety of areas without appearing arrogant or condescending is a difficult yet worthwhile balance to achieve. Competence shows knowledge, experience, adaptability, and the willingness to learn. A leader's confidence naturally grows over time as he consistently exercises good judgment, makes sound decisions, and achieves measurable goals.

The ability to inspire others is often inherent to charismatic leaders. Many people naturally want to follow their example and believe in their message. Leaders lacking natural charisma must learn to compensate through improved communication and interpersonal skills. The greatest ideas are worthless unless or until they are communicated to others in ways that generate excitement, incite passion, and create hope. Successful leaders study the ways others communicate and listen carefully to the people around them. They hone their people-reading skills and learn how to push emotional buttons. They are experts in disseminating information in ways that stimulate listeners and provoke desired reactions. The ability to inspire others comes easier to some, but it can be learned by most. This trait is one to display carefully. Beating people over the head with superior knowledge is counterproductive. Indeed, in all communications it is best to stick with a clear message, using simple language that is understood across a broad audience. Demonstrating a willingness and ability to engage in continuous learning goes further toward demonstrating intelligence than does always having the right answer. Intelligence is critical to building confidence because without a solid knowledge base, it is impossible to make good decisions and act competently. On the same note, we gain the confidence of others by respecting their intelligence as well.

The GLOBE studies identify several universally desirable characteristics of outstanding leaders, one of which is building confidence. Across cultures and industries, the ability to build confidence is critical to success in leadership. A team is only as strong as its weakest link. True leaders inspire others to feel better about themselves, to perform better than they ever have in the past, and to reach for higher goals. Great leaders share in celebrating successes and instigate the quick resolution of problems. Excellent leaders teach each of their followers to find their strengths and put them to use in accomplishing the shared goal or vision.

Conclusion

Cultural leadership exposes a leader to rare magic that causes the young, the old, men, women, rich, and poor to look around and recognize they stand together for one goal, one purpose, and under the guidance of one leader. Cultural leadership, when done effectively, is supported by a transportable chemistry that plants cultural seeds by prioritizing the creation of chemistry between members, translating this chemistry into meaningful action and a sense of impact. This is how cultural leadership is born, developed, and sustained.

Cultural leadership is an entire culture in and of itself, one that reflects rather than imposes. It begins with a blank canvas onto which multiple cultures can paint their concerns and closely held beliefs. Cultural leadership is a mirror, one that reflects one person at a time. It is intimate. It is personal. Global connectedness has lengthened the reach of business, education, and social understanding. The only thing left is for leaders to respond in kind.

Traditional leadership theory says to remove personal feelings from business. This is a flawed concept. With more options comes a greater participation of feelings in day-to-day consumer decisions. In essence, the new model for leadership through cultural leadership is: "It's not business, it's just personal."

Acknowledgments

I want to thank my family for their continued support through this long and rewarding process. I would also like to thank my clients, who have provided much of the insight contained within this book. Of special thanks goes to the men and women of the Army and Air National Guard who have consistently provided a laboratory of fresh and innovative thinking, which moved this project along.

References

Aliber, R.Z. & Click, R.W. (1971). *The multinational enterprise in a multiple currency world.* In J.H. Dunning (Eds),George Allen & Unwin, London.

Anderson, Philip. (1999). Seven Levers for Guiding the Evolving Enterprise. in John Henry Clippinger III (ed.) *The Biology of Business: Decoding the Natural Laws of Enterprise,* 113–152. San Francisco: Jossey-Bass.

Baldoni, J. (2003). *Great communication secrets of great leaders.* New York: McGraw-Hill.

Bass, B., & Avolio, B. (1994). *Improving Organizational Effectiveness Through Transformational Leadership.* Thousand Oaks, CA: Sage Publications.

Beyer, J.M. (1999). Taming and promoting charisma to change organizations.

Leadership Quarterly, 10(2), 307–330.

Boal, K.B. & Bryson, J.M. (1988). *Charismatic leadership: A phenomenological and structural approach.* Pp. 528 in J.G. Hunt, B.R. Baliga, H.P Dachler & C.A. Schriesheim

(Eds.), Emerging leadership vistas. Lexington, MA: Lexington Books

Branam, K.D. (2003). Perception is reality. *Texas Law Reporter*, 2(2), Retrieved from http://www.branam.com/ makingsense/kdb_texaslawreporter.pdf

Burns, J. M. (1978). *Leadership*. New York: Harper & Row. Staff Writers. (2007, February 12). My year at Wal-mart: How marketing whiz Julie Roehm suffered a spectacular fall in 10 short months. *Business Week*, Retrieved from http://www.businessweek.com/ magazine/content/07_07/b4021076.htm

Camarota, S.A., & McArdle, N. (2003). Where immigrants live: an examination of state residency of the foreign born by country of origin in 1990 and 2000. *Center for Immigration Studies*, Retrieved from http://www.ci.org/ImmigrantsStateResidency

Carte & Fox. (2004). *Bridging the culture gap.* Kogan Page Ltd.

Clippinger, J.H. (1999). *The biology of business: decoding the natural laws of enterprise.* San Francisco: Jossey Bass.

Denning, S. (2004). *Squirrel inc.: A fable of leadership through storytelling.* San Francisco, CA: Jossey-Bass.

Fast Company Staff, Initials. (2008, November 25). Cisco's CEO John Chambers on how to weather the downturn. *Fast Company*, (131), Retrieved from http://www.fastcompany .com/magazine/131/what-would-john-do.html   Staff Writers. (2008, February 4). 100 Best companies to work for. *Fortune* magazine, Retrieved from http://money.cnn .com/magazines/fortune/bestcompanies/2008/full_list/ind ex.html

Friedman, T.L. (2006). *The world is flat: a brief history of the twenty-first century.* USA: Farrar, Straus & Giroux.

Gladwell, M. (2000). *The tipping point: How little things can make a big difference.* Little Brown and Company.

Godin, S. (2008). *Tribes: We need you to lead us.* New York: Portfolio Publications.

Goldberg, L.R. (1992). The development of markers for the big-five factor structure. *Journal of Personality and Social Psychology,* 59(6), 1216–1229.

Gregersen, H. B., Morrison, A. J. & Black, J. S. (1998). Developing leaders for the global frontier. Sloan Management Review, 40(1), 21–33.

Hamel, G. & Prahalad, C.K. (1996). *Competing for the future.* Harvard Business School Press.

Hannum, K.M. (2007). *Social identity: knowing yourself, leading others.* North Carolina: Center for Creative Leadership.

Hitt, M.A., Ireland, R.D., & Hoskisson, R.E. (1999). *Strategic management: Competitiveness & globalization.* Thompson.

Holland, J.H. (1998). *Emergence: From chaos to order.* Reading, MA: Addison-Wesley.

Ibarra, H, & Hunter, M. (2007, January). How leaders create and use networks. *Harvard Business Review,* Retrieved from http://hbr.harvardbusiness.org/2007/01/how-leaders-create-and-use-networks/ar/1

Jarvenpaa, S.L. & Leidner, D.E. (1998). *Communication and trust in global virtual teams.*

Kawamoto, D., & Krazit, T. (2006, September 5). Media leaks prompt HP board shake up. *CNET News,* Retrieved from http://news.cnet.com/Media-leaks-prompt-HP-board-shake-up/21---1014_3-6112501.html?tag=mncol

Kouzes, J. and Posner, B. *The Leadership Challenge.* San Francisco:　　　　　　　　　　　Jossey-Bass 2000.

Lane, H.W., DiStefano, J.J., & Maznevski, M.L. (2000). *International management behavior: Text, readings, & cases.* Blackwell Publishing Ltd.

Levick, R.S. (2006, December 1). Water rising: Minimizing the damage from corporate leaks. *HG.Org Worldwide Legal Directories.* Retrieved from http://www.levick.com/resources/topics/articles/water_rising.php

Lechner, F. (2000–2001). *What is globalization?* Retrieved from http://www.sociology.emory.edu/globalization/issues01.html

Liverum Research Group. Retrieved from *http://liberum.twst.com*

Lohr, S. (2007, July 18). I.B.M. showing that giants can be nimble. *New York Times.* C1.

Martin, A., Willburn, P., Morrow, P., Downing, K., & Criswell, C. (2007). What's next? The 2007 changing nature of leadership survey. *A CCL Research White Paper,* Retrieved from https://www.ccl.org/leadership/pdf/research/WhatsNext.pdf

McCrae, R.R. & Costa, P.T. (1990). *Personality in adulthood.* New York: The Guildford Press.

McFarlin, D. & Sweeney, P. (2005). *International management: Strategic opportunities & cultural challenges.* Cengage.

Merriam-Webster. (1983). Trust. *Websters ninth new collegiate dictionary.* Springfield, MA: Merriam-Webster.

Misztal, B. (1996). *Trust in modern societies.* Cambridge, UK: Polity Press.

Norman, W.T. (1963). Toward an adequate taxonomy of personality attributes: Replicated factor structure in peer nomination personality ratings. *Journal of Abnormal and Social Psychology*, (66), 574–583.

Pearce, C.L. & Conger, J.A. (2003). *Shared Leadership: Reframing the How and Whys of Leadership*. Thousand Oaks, CA: Sage Publications.

Pietersen, W. (2002). *Reinventing strategy: Using strategic learning to create and sustain breakthrough performance*. New York: John Wiley & Sons, Inc.

Robinson, P. (2008). [Interview with Shelby Steele, author of A bound man: Why we are excited about Obama and why he can't win].

Rooke, D. & Torbert, W.R. (2005, April). Seven transformations of leadership. *Harvard Business Review*.

Seltzer, J. & Bass, B. (1990). Transformational leadership beyond initiation and consideration. *Journal of Management, (*16), *693–703*.

Slaughter, R. (1995). *The foresight principle: Cultural recovery in the 21st century*. Connecticut: Praeger Publishers.

Stephenson, K. (2006). *The quantum theory of trust: Power, networks and the secret life of organizations*. Canada: Pearson Education.

Stitt, J. (2008, August 14). CIO leadership series: Tim Schaefer, Northwestern Mutual. *FusionCIO*, Retrieved from http://wistechnology.com/fusioncio/article/4931/

Sen, A. (2004, October). Interdependence and global justice. Speech presented at the general Assembly of the United Nations.

Schein, E.H. (1985). *Organizational Culture and Leadership*. San Francisco: Jossey-Bass Publishers.

Spence, G. (1996). *How to argue and win every time*. New York, NY: St. Martin's Griffin.

Steele, S. (2008). *A bound man: Why we are excited about Obama and why he can't win*. New York: Free Press.

Stellin, S. (2001, May 16). Cultures Clash as AOL switches to its email. *The New York Times*.

Taras, V., Rowney, J., & Steel, P. (2005). Cross-cultural differences and dynamics of culture over time: A meta-analysis of hofstede's taxonomy. Paper presented at the Academy of Management Conference, Honolulu, HI.

Watkins, M. (2003). *The First 90 Days: Critical Success Strategies for New Leaders at All Levels.* Harvard Business School Press.

Whitelaw, K. & Omestad, T. (2004, November 21). The new face at foggy bottom: Condoleezza Rice has Bush's ear, but can she sell his ideas abroad? *U.S. News & World Report*, Retrieved from http://www.usnews.com/usnews/news/articles/041129/29rice.htm

Made in United States
Orlando, FL
03 December 2021

11092920R00085